Three Compulsions

THAT Defeat Most Men

Vincent Gallagher, M.A.

BETHANY HOUSE PUBLISHERS
MINNEAPOLIS, MINNESOTA 55438

Published by Bethany House Publishers
A Ministry of Bethany Fellowship, Inc.
6820 Auto Club Road, Minneapolis, Minnesota 55438

Printed in the United States of America

Library of Congress Cataloging-in-Publication Data

Gallagher, Vincent G.
    Three compulsions that defeat most men / Vincent G. Gallagher
       p. cm.
Includes bibliographical references
1. Men—Religious life. 2. Compulsive behavior—Religious aspects—Christianity. 3. Workaholism. 4. Substance abuse. 5. Sex addiction. I. Title
BV4843.G35   1992
248.8'42—dc20   92–36012
ISBN 1–55661–275–3   CIP

Three Compulsions THAT Defeat Most Men

This book is dedicated
to Amy Patricia,
my friend, my partner, my wife.

VINCENT GALLAGHER is a Christian counselor with Life Counseling Services, a large Christian counseling center located in suburban Philadelphia. He conducts individual, marriage, family, and group therapy, specializing in compulsivity, marriage counseling, and men's issues. He is a frequent speaker at churches, schools, and seminars in the Philadelphia area.

He earned his master's degree in counseling at Denver Conservative Baptist Seminary in Denver, Colorado, and an undergraduate degree in youth ministry at Eastern College in St. David's, Pennsylvania.

His favorite pastime is being with his wife and daughter.

CONTENTS

1
WAITING FOR THE MIRACLE WORKER

The newspapers carried big, bold headlines announcing the event.

The nightly newscast devoted five minutes to it.

It was certainly the biggest event this little town had seen in a long, long time.

"The miracle worker" was coming to town.

As John lay in his bed, reading all about it, he felt conflicting emotions begin to stir within him. *If only I could meet this man,* he thought. *If all of the things they're saying about him are true. . . .*

But the minute his spirits began to rise, reality set in.

That's really dumb, he thought miserably. *I can hardly move—I'm hardly even a "man" anymore.*

After the paralyzing accident his body had become nearly useless. Day after day, he'd tried, with every ounce of strength and concentration he could muster, to get one little finger or toe to move. And he couldn't. And he finally gave up. After five years . . . shouldn't he learn to just accept his condition? Things weren't ever going to change— and it was far past time that he faced that fact.

While he was sinking into another black mood, the door burst open.

Four men—one of them was his brother, Matt—came over to his bedside.

"Come on, John," Matt said, "we're going to take you for a little ride. The miracle worker's in town. We're going to take you to him."

"But I . . ."

"Oh, come on," one of the others teased. "Do you have something better to do?"

In a short time, they were pulling up in front of the civic auditorium where the miracle worker was appearing.

As soon as he saw the crowd in front of the place, John's heart sank. There was no way to get in. Not only was the place packed, but the crowd spilled out of every entrance, and even the parking lot was full of people.

"What now?" one of the men asked.

No one said anything for a moment. And then Matt pointed to a fire escape, leading up to an upper story—and a door.

And so it was, a few minutes later, that John found himself being jostled up narrow stairs and inside through backstage hallways—right into the presence of the miracle worker . . . not to mention the huge audience crowded into the auditorium.

But the miracle worker turned his compassionate gaze onto the face of the paralyzed man himself, seeing far beyond his crippled body, and into his crippled soul.

"Son," he said, "your sins are forgiven."

A skeptic in the front row shouted out, "Sins *schmins*. What's that got to do with anything?"

"Sins?" someone else yelled. "You can't have your sins forgiven unless you've been baptized!"

"That's right," another cried. "Or at least until you've gone forward during an altar call!"

The miracle worker just smiled . . . a sad, weary smile.

"You don't understand," he said. "This man's body is bound, yes. But his soul . . . his mind . . . this is where the real paralysis lies."

Then, turning his attention to John, the miracle worker said, "I want you to be free from *everything* that binds you.

"Get up. Be whole . . . and go on home."

The story you have just read is true . . . with some obvious "tweaks." You can read about it in the second chapter of Mark in the New Testament. The miracle worker's name, of course, is Jesus Christ. One of the things that has always amazed me about this account is that Jesus looked right past the man's crippled body and into his crippled soul. He saw that this aspect of his being, more than anything else, was where healing was needed.

You just can't tell what's going on in a man by looking at the surface.

There are many men walking around today who look completely strong and healthy—but underneath it all, their minds and souls are crippled—paralyzed by fear, sorrow, and compulsion.

They've tried to get free by following various religious formulas:

• Pray more.
• Read the Bible more.
• Believe harder.

But none of these things have brought them freedom.

In moments of despair, they may wish for a miracle man.

In C. S. Lewis's *The Great Divorce,* Lewis invents a demonic "lizard of lust" who has his sharp claws buried deeply in his victims. As soon as the lizard is thrust through with a sword, the victim is set free from his compulsive, lustful attitudes.

Wouldn't it be great if that was the way it worked, if someone could come along with a sharp sword and kill the creatures that hold us captive?

But for some of us it has been a long, long wait, and no one has come along to slay our lizards and set us free.

Some of us don't understand why we're overtaken by powerful urges that we can't seem to control. Why we can't control our compulsions to engage in promiscuous sex, drink to excess, or spend all our time working, while our interpersonal relationships, left unattended, wither and die.

Are you bound by some particular feeling or behavior that you'd like to get rid of?

Are you like the paralyzed man in the story who feels defeated? Have you tried to gain control but found that you are powerless to change for very long? Then, perhaps the way in which you view the problem is part of the problem itself. It is time to experience the grace of God that can truly set you free from your self-conscious efforts to change.

If we focus on the behavior, we are only seeing the tip of the iceberg. What we have to do is look down deep into the soul, to see what's *causing* that behavior . . . the way Jesus looked past the paralyzed man's body, and into his heart and soul.

That's what we're going to do in this book.

We're going to take a journey far below the surface, and into the depths of life. In the process, we're going to learn some things about ourselves.

And before the journey is through, we are going to uncover the reasons behind our behaviors that keep us from being all God has destined us to be. And we are going to see how to strengthen our relationships with our friends, our families, and God.

2
A NEW WAY OF LOOKING
AT LIFE

Are you a compulsive person?

Ask a question like that and you're probably going to get an indignant answer. If the person you're asking is a man, the answer you get might go beyond polite indignation into surliness.

"Me . . . compulsive? Of course not."

You see, one of the myths of our society is that we men are extremely rational in the things we say and do. We think everything through before we act, and then we take the logical, rational choice. Webster defines compulsion as "an irresistible impulse to perform an irrational act." And that's just not the way men are.

That, at least, is the way the myth goes. But that's all it is. A myth. The truth is that all human beings are susceptible to compulsive behavior, even men. Even Christian men.

Far too many Christian men are bound by compulsions, and thus kept from being all God wants them to be. In this book, we are going to dialogue about the journey to spiritual wholeness and maturity. We're going to face compulsions that bind us, and consider the steps to the kind of freedom that Christ wants us to have.

Why do we sometimes behave in ways that don't make sense? In most instances it is because that's what we have been *trained* to do. We behave compulsively because it's a way to medicate a deep pain—a pain that has become so deep it feels like emotional and spiritual numbness.

Do you feel hurt or out of control or stressed out in

some way? You're certainly not alone. The fact that there are some 300,000 psychotherapeutic professionals in the United States gives testimony to the fact that you have many fellow strugglers.[1]

Still, far too many Christian men today are afraid to be honest, with their wives, their Christian friends, and even with themselves. They know deep down that there are areas where they need help, but they won't admit it. And so they hide behind masks of piety and perfection, pretending to be what they're not.

But it is time to stop pretending, admit our weaknesses, and begin to understand our fallen humanity and our utter need to depend on God and His grace.

If you are a man who realizes that he struggles with certain areas of his life, if you want to begin healing and grow in Christ, then please keep reading.

Specifically, I will discuss three areas where men—even good Christian men—may become trapped in compulsive, destructive behavior.

The areas of a man's life where he is most vulnerable are:

1. work
2. sex
3. alcohol

What about *your* work life? Does your wife think you're spending far too much time at the office these days? Do you think about work even when you're supposed to be relaxing with your family? Does it just about kill you to go on a vacation away from the office? If you recognize yourself in any of these situations, or if you simply feel that your work life has gotten too much of a hold over you— help *is* available.

And what about your sex life? Is it out of control? Perhaps you have difficulty controlling your fantasy life. Maybe you have trouble being faithful to your wife. Or it could be that you want to have a healthier approach to sex in general and women in particular, but you can't seem to help yourself. Perhaps you don't think you have a *big* problem in this area, but you'd like to be *purer in heart*. If any of these descriptions fit you, I want to assure you, you *can* change.

And then there's alcohol. Does it have a stronger hold on you than you'd really care to admit? Do you tell yourself that you don't really *need* to drink or that you could quit anytime—but keep on drinking anyway? You will learn how your compulsions are keeping you from experiencing the legitimate pain that you have buried. If you will deal with the deeper pain, your compulsivity will lessen, but it will be a long process. Part of the compulsive mentality is the desire for a "quick fix." We can also bring that need into misguided efforts at controlling ourselves. But there is no "quick fix" to help us stop being compulsive. Getting better and staying better is a lifetime process of honesty and humility. Growth and maturity come when we begin to admit our pain and learn to live with it instead of covering it through compulsions that make us feel good temporarily.

We have been taught that pain is always bad. So we try to avoid it at all cost. Yet, life is naturally painful, and the pain we feel can lead us closer to God if we will face it and stop turning to the idols of our "quick fixes."

Living in a World of Confusion

A great many men today are confused regarding the proper approach to work, sex, and alcohol, and this confusion has compounded naturally compulsive behavior.

Confusion is to be expected, because in a lot of ways this is a difficult time to be a man—whether or not you're a Christian. Why? Because today's man lives in a world of paradoxes. He is supposed to be tough, but he's also supposed to be tender. He's supposed to work hard and be a good provider, but not so hard that he can't always be there when his family needs him. He's supposed to be a "take charge" guy who's always ready to make the tough decision, but he's also expected to take everyone else's feelings and wishes into consideration when he makes that decision. If he watches television at all, he probably thinks it's perfectly natural to head for "Miller Time" at the end of a hard day's work, or to believe that "it doesn't get any better" than sharing a few beers with a group of good friends. But he's never, ever supposed to drink too much—and if he's a Christian who doesn't drink at all, he's probably tempted by all those beautiful, happy people in beer commercials to think that he's really missing out on something.

Add to that, our society's seeming preoccupation with physical perfection. Author-counselor John Bradshaw says, "Our society presents a physical perfectionistic system which is cruelly shaming to the physically unendowed . . . The perfect "10" man has a muscular, tanned, and pro-portionately perfect physical body. . . . These physical ideals have caused untold suffering and shame to an incredible number of people."[2]

No wonder so many men are confused about themselves and the role they're supposed to play in life.

In the sexual area of life, for instance, the male is by his very nature more aggressive. He is expected to be the one who pursues the female. It is natural for him to be the one who initiates sexual contact.

If you are a married man, ask yourself how many times—out of the last ten times you and your wife made love—you initiated the act. Chances are very good, if yours is a typical marriage, that you "made the first move" more than half the time. Probably quite a bit more than half the time. There's no problem with that. It doesn't mean your wife doesn't find you appealing. It merely means that you are the more aggressive one—and that is exactly what your nature calls you to be.

But the problem for too many men is that their aggressive nature in sexual matters goes into overdrive. They may find that, instead of them being in control of their sex drive, their sex drive is in control of them.

And compulsive sexual behavior is *not* limited to the unchristian world—no matter how much those of us who are Christians hate to admit that this sort of behavior is found in the church.

Just a few days ago, I heard about a church where the senior pastor was forced to resign after it was discovered that he was having affairs with *several* married women in his congregation. Here is a man with a long career as a pastor, a man who became a minister of the gospel because he wanted to reach people with the love of Christ. But a man who has allowed his sexual compulsion to compromise his witness, perhaps destroy him, and maybe his church, too.

It's not the first time I've heard a story like that, and I know it won't be the last.

But the only reason we hear about a pastor who falls into sexual sin is because he's up there in the limelight—like a baseball player whose errors are printed in the next day's paper for the entire world to see.

The rest of us may not get the notoriety, or the headlines, but our compulsions can be just as destructive and just as troubling.

When I think of the three most common compulsions—work, sex, and alcohol—I immediately think of three men who came to me for counsel. Their names were Dan, Bill, and Tony.

Please pay close attention as I tell you the stories of these men—and please think carefully about your reaction. What I really want you to do as you hear their stories is think about yourself. Do you see any of their weaknesses in your life? And if so, how do you handle those weaknesses?

Some of us get so busy with judging other people that we can't see our own shortcomings. But it's only by seeing our own failures, and understanding the underlying *reasons* for those failures, that we can move toward spiritual wholeness. So read carefully, and see if you recognize any of your own tendencies in the stories of these three men: Dan . . . Bill . . . and Tony.

DAN

Dan didn't even think he had a problem. He had only come to see me because his wife insisted upon it. He let me know that right away.

"I'll get right to the point. I'm not sure exactly what needs to be done about it, but my wife thinks I work too much. She probably saw something on the *Oprah Winfrey Show.*" He rolled his eyes at the mention of Oprah.

"So anyway . . . I'm here because I told her I'd come to counseling. It was really just to get her off my back."

He didn't have to tell me that. Because of his defensive posture, it had been obvious from the minute he walked in my door.

When I probed a little bit about his work habits, he became more than a bit defensive.

"Sure I work hard. And long, too! I built my business with my bare hands, no help from anyone, and I'm worth plenty now." With more than a hint of anger in his voice, he said of his wife, "She never used to mind it before our youngest left for college."

He told me that he had tried to cut his hours in an effort to appease his wife. He was still spending about seventy hours per week on the job, but he figured that was the absolute minimum to keep things running smoothly.

"My business demands it," he said when I asked if maybe his minimum work week of seventy hours was still a bit too much. "Besides, if you want something done right, you have to do it yourself."

Dan's argument seemed pretty good, but there was one thing that gave him away: the way his eyes lit up when he talked about his business. It was obviously the central theme of his life—far more important to him than his marriage, his wife, or his children.

But if it came down to choosing between his business and his marriage, I wasn't sure what he would do.

BILL

The first time Bill entered my office, he was dressed neatly in his tie and white shirt. He had come directly from his office, where he managed business accounts for a national insurance firm. As he sat down and looked across the desk at me, I immediately noticed the look of desperation in his eyes.

"I need help," he began. "I've tried everything. Nothing works."

"Can you tell me what you're struggling with?" I asked.

"I think I'm out of control . . . uh . . . sexually."

"Tell me what you mean," I said.

He squirmed uncomfortably in his seat.

"Well . . ." He stopped to clear his throat. "I can't seem to stop thinking about it. My fantasy life is totally out of control."

"I see."

"And lately . . . well . . . I've been masturbating. Quite a bit."

He sat back and looked at me nervously, as if he thought I might order him to get out of my office. Instead, I just urged him to keep talking.

"After I masturbate, I say to myself that it was the last time . . . that I'm going to stop, but it seems like I always go back to it. I've tried everything! My wife thinks I'm compulsive . . . and maybe I am. I seem to overdo a lot of things."

I asked him if he had talked to anyone else about his problem.

"I talked to my pastor, and he told me to stop it, but the temptations won't go away. I guess I feel like a failure spiritually." He punctuated that last statement with a deep sigh, and a brief shake of his head.

"What are you feeling right now?" I asked.

"Like I said . . . I feel like a failure. I just can't stop. I ask God for forgiveness, but my pastor said that if I go back to it then I must not really be sorry."

He paused for a moment.

"But I *am* sorry," he finally said. "And I hate myself when I do it."

TONY

And then there was Tony.

Tony had deep, black lines of grease on his hands. I knew that he was an auto mechanic before he even told me what he did for a living.

In contrast to Bill's dress shirt and expensive tie, Tony wore jeans, a pair of black work boots, and a blue workshirt with his name embroidered on one pocket. He slumped down in his chair, holding his head in his hands.

"I blew it again, man," he said. "I swore I'd never drink again, but then sure enough, two months later I'm making a fool of myself in front of my family."

He was obviously in emotional pain as he went on, "I just don't understand it. My friends can take a couple of drinks, and then they stop. With me, well, you never know what I'm going to do after I have that first beer. Sometimes I'm able to stop after three or four . . . and sometimes I keep drinking all night until I'm blitzed."

That wasn't all.

"And I never know what mood I'm gonna be in after I start drinking."

"What are you feeling right now?" I asked.

"Bummed out. Depressed. Disappointed."

I urged him to go on.

"Yeah, my wife took me to this Bible study thing a couple of months ago, after my last binge. This dude there cast some demons out of me and everything. He said that I was being oppressed by 'the spirit of alcohol,' and he wanted to cast it out, so I let him. I mean, you know, I figured it couldn't hurt anything, and I was hoping it was going to do me some good." He shook his head. "Obviously it didn't."

Thinking back to that Bible study, Tony remembered how happy his wife had been. She just knew that her husband wasn't going to drink again. For two months, he had done his best to live up to her expectations, but now he had let her down.

He sighed, "I was all set to stay sober forever. I *really* wanted to . . . I guess I need to go get deliverance again. This demon is really on my back."

Dan, Bill, and Tony. Three men with three different compulsions . . . and all getting wrong answers about the sources of and solutions to those compulsions.

Bill and Tony knew they were "overdoing" something.

Deep down, Dan probably knew, too, although he didn't want to admit it. But none of these men really knew *why* they did what they did, or how they could stop it.

Bill was told, "Just stop it," by his pastor.

Dan thought he had to work so hard because "a real man has to pull himself up by his own bootstraps."

Tony was told that he wasn't responsible for his own actions, because "the devil made you do it." And, furthermore, "If you cast out the demon, you'll be fine."

These are just a few of several wrong approaches men can choose from to help explain why they do the things they do—*and* what they can do to change things. Anyone who's looking for an excuse can find one, and he won't have to look that hard. Unfortunately, if you have an excuse, you don't need to dig deeper to find the real causes for your behavior, or make a real effort to change.

In chapter 3, we're going to take a closer look at some of these wrong approaches to life.

3

WELL-MEANING ADVICE—
BUT WRONG

This is the age of the instant: When something news-worthy happens, anywhere in the world, we can count on CNN to bring immediate reports into our living room.

It's easy to think that there ought to be a simple and quick answer to everything.

Unfortunately, the world doesn't really work that way.

People don't work that way.

The work of spiritual wholeness takes time. Building interpersonal relationships takes time. Developing the skill of empathy, of compassionate listening to others, takes time.

Sadly, many men who are seeking to overcome the compulsions that bind them—men like Dan, Bill, and Tony—are often kept from making true progress by following wrong approaches to their difficulties. They want quick and easy answers, when the true answers are long in coming—and therefore long-lasting.

I want to discuss some of the wrong approaches men often use to justify their irrational or compulsive behavior—along with some of the simplistic solutions they get from well-meaning friends.

We need to talk about these wrong ways of thinking that can actually stifle growth and keep a man bound by his compulsion.

The Just-Do-It Approach. This approach simply tells the struggler to "just stop" his wrong behavior. It's like the NIKE shoe commercial says, "Just do it." Only it's not that simple. This is the approach that Bill's pastor took when dealing with him about his compulsive sexual behavior.

"Just stop it, Bill. And if you don't stop it, you must not be truly sorry."

That sort of approach rarely helps, and it often hurts by piling guilt on top of guilt.

Are you trying to quit smoking? Just stop. Drinking? Quit. Are you addicted to drugs? Don't take them anymore. Those who preach this model think that if you don't stop—drinking, smoking, or whatever else the wrong behavior might be—then you must be rebellious. If you keep falling into sin, that means you haven't truly repented.

"All you need to do," the compulsive person is told, "is read the Bible more, pray more, and stop sinning. After all, if you would just stop focusing on yourself so much and start doing something to serve others, then you could die to 'self.' "

The primary flaw of the Just-Do-It Approach is the simple fact that believers are still human. And all humans often miss the mark, even those who have faith and the Spirit of Christ dwelling within them. Compulsivity is universal. A man who seeks to follow Christ is still going to suffer temptation, and he is still going to struggle and fall when he tries to rely on "soul-medicating" practices in which there is no real healing. The Bible advises Christians to "confess your sins to each other and pray for each other so that you may be healed."[1] That compassionate, understanding, and prayerful attitude is a far cry from the approach taken by those who say, "Just stop it."

Too many people in our churches develop an attitude that is basically anti-Christian. They think just because they have overcome a few outward sinful behaviors they are somehow holier than others who still struggle. Yet they are self-deceived if they don't realize that they are falling prey to the sin of spiritual pride.

Legalism has always been a problem in the church. Why do people have such a hard time with receiving God's grace and giving it out to others? Basically, the prideful heart wants to take a little bit of credit for its gains in holiness. This attitude puffs one up and leads to becoming critical of others who don't measure up. The difference between the spirit of legalism and the spirit of grace is that the latter leads to a fuller love of God, self, and others, while the former leads to pride, judgmentalism, self-righteousness, and hypocrisy. It's time to stop judging and controlling one another and begin to love and accept with the compassion of Jesus.

The Tough-Guy Approach. Dan fell victim to this type of thinking. His wife just didn't understand that men *have* to work seventy, eighty or ninety hours a week to provide for their families.

This approach also says that real men don't express pain. They endure it in silence. A real man learns to "bite the bullet," grit his teeth, and never let anyone know how bad it hurts.

A great many people fall victim to this kind of thinking, sometimes in very dangerous ways. For example, consider the difference between men and women with regard to going to the doctor. When a woman gets sick, if she doesn't get over it in a few days she'll probably go to the doctor. But a man will let something drag on for days, even weeks, and he won't even *consider* going to the doctor.

"Just another couple of days," he says. "If I don't feel better by then, I'll go in and get checked out." And he'll keep saying the same thing over and over. Usually, the only way he'll actually go to the doctor is if he's married and his wife insists on it.

Why do men behave that way? Because they have been trained to believe that this is the way they are supposed to be.

My father, a big game hunter, once went on a hunting trip with a close friend. In spite of their closeness, however, my father's companion never told him or anyone else that he had serious heart problems. And so, in the middle of the hunt, miles away from civilization, this man had a heart attack and died before help could arrive.

I'm not saying that his life could have been saved if he had been more honest about his condition. But certainly, preparations could have been made that would have made his survival more likely. There's a decision to be made. Sometimes it's a decision that has to do with life and death. Always it's a decision of importance. Should I be a "tough-guy" type of character and deny that I have any weakness or problems—and perhaps even die prematurely as a result? Or is it more manly to face up to my own pain and try to deal with it—even if it means admitting my weaknesses to some people and enlisting their help?

Obviously, the second approach makes more sense.

The "Devil-Made-Me-Do-It" Approach. This approach to life believes that all compulsivity must be the work of a demon. And if that's the case, then all you have to do to change your behavior is to cast out the demon—and then you'll be fine.

It's easy to see why so many people like this. It absolves them from responsibility, and it holds out the promise of a quick fix. I know that the Devil and his demons exist. And I believe they do everything within their power to get people to do things that displease God. And often demonic influence can be an influence in compulsive behavior. Demons can and do tempt, harass, and oppress believers. The ministry of deliverance is an important gift to the church and a much needed one. However, too many well-meaning people unlearned in the behavioral sciences can and do confuse emotional problems with demonic infestation. Not all unpleasant feelings and inner conflict are caused by demons. The "demon-under-every-bush" mentality smacks of ignorance, paranoia, and lack of discernment. It would be nice if we could just rebuke all our problems away. To the compulsive desirous of a pain-free quick fix, the promise of serenity after a quick prayer is indeed enticing. Yet, true change and growth often takes struggle, pain, and time. The deliverance ministry has been profoundly abused.

Once, I heard about an overweight man who had the "spirit of M&M's" cast out of him. I've always wondered which kind left easier—plain . . . or peanuts.

Now, please don't misunderstand and think that I'm poking fun at the ministry of deliverance. I know there is a place for such a ministry, but I also believe it takes a special and uncommon gift of discernment to identify real demonic oppression. And, even when there *is* demonic attack, the Enemy only hits where there is already a weakness or a wound. Until the wound is healed, evil will find a resonance within.

The "Never-Follow-a-Woman" Approach. Some men wouldn't follow a woman if she were leading them out of a burning building. Dan, our compulsive worker, wasn't like that. But he was close. He dismissed his wife's anger as being silly, and couldn't understand for all the world why she couldn't see things his way. Of course, he didn't make a bit of effort to see things *her* way.

Some men believe that they should never listen to any voice that challenges them to look within—especially if that voice belongs to a woman. To listen to a woman is to admit weakness. And to admit weakness is a great taboo. It doesn't even matter, really, if what the woman says is true. It's going to be discounted, just because *she* said it.

Men who refuse to listen to women are running from something. What they need to do, more than anything else, is engage in true dialogue with the women in their lives, especially their wives. At the same time, the woman herself needs to strive to understand that differences between the sexes are more than physical—that they also extend into the ways men and women communicate, the ways they respond to various stimuli, etc.

The fault does not always lie with the husband; the wife must be very careful that she is not shaming her husband for displaying natural male characteristics that are alien to her style or values.

The modern male really is on the horns of a dilemma. He is sometimes shamed by his own cultural myths that tell him he has to behave like John Wayne or Rambo; and at other times he is shamed by women who don't understand what it means to be male. (And it is not at all uncommon that a woman will harbor unconscious rage at her father, a rage that invariably gets projected onto the second most important man in her life: her husband.)

But again, an important thing for men to keep in mind is that it's all right to learn from a woman, to let her teach you, to react positively when she tells you something that you know is true.

The Magic-Thinking Approach. It would be a terrific life indeed if this approach really worked. All a man would have to do would be to wish for something—or pray for something—and he would have it.

"Dear Lord, please help me win the lottery tomorrow, Amen." And you would. But then, why bother with the lottery? All you'd really have to say is, "Lord, I could really use a million bucks," and it would fall out of the sky, landing with a loud crash, right beside you. If there was anything about yourself that you wanted to change, you could say a few words, snap your fingers, and everything would be fine.

Of course, I'm taking this way of thinking to its extreme, but this is pretty close to the attitude I've encountered in some Christians. They have accepted a "name-it-and-claim-it" theology. They think, "If only I can muster up enough faith, my life is going to be wonderful." "If I visualize myself becoming successful it is certainly going to happen." And so on.

The weak foundation of this approach lies in another theological error. You cannot control God by saying the "right" words. You're not the one in charge here—*He* is!

Just as you cannot control God, neither can you control others by speaking the right words. This approach betrays a controlling nature on the part of the practitioner. The Christian who is truly yielded to and trusting in God will want to surrender his life to God's will, rather than seeking to control God, other people, or events by obsessive spiritual pronouncements.

These, then, are some of the erroneous approaches to life that men live by.

But if a man is ever going to grow into maturity and become the person God intended him to be, he has to develop a new way of looking at things.

There is a better way.

You don't need to deny your problems or project them onto demons. There is a more masculine, authentic way to deal with your pain. For to be truly masculine is to be able to face up to your pain and learn to deal with it in an appropriate and healthy manner.

A New Approach. In chapter 2, I introduced you to three men who had different compulsions—different behavior problems.

Bill was obsessed with sex and pornography.

Dan was a workaholic who was about to lose his wife as a result.

Tony couldn't seem to stop drinking no matter how many demons he had cast out of him.

But you see, in each of these men the behavior was not the real problem. The behavior was only the symptom of the problem. All of them were hiding from pain. The things they did were medicating the hurt that came from some deep wound somewhere in their lives.

Some compulsive drinkers are honest enough with themselves that they can admit they're drinking to hide their pain. That type of honesty is rare among those whose lives are dominated by a compulsion related to work . . . but primarily because most of them have never given a second thought to why they work so hard or so long. When I asked Dan if he had ever considered the fact that work was like a drug to him, he acted as if he couldn't possibly understand what I meant. But the more we talked about it, the more he began to see my point.

Are you like Dan? Are you *medicating* your pain through momentary pleasures that make you feel better for a while, but which lead you into habitual sin and, therefore, self-condemnation? Perhaps it's time for you to look at the pain that fuels these compulsions.

M. Scott Peck, in his best-selling work, *The Road Less Traveled*, said that the "tendency to avoid problems and the emotional suffering inherent in them is the primary basis of all human mental illness."[2] Facing up to pain can be difficult. But in the final analysis, pain is not the problem. Refusing to face up to pain, or dealing with it incorrectly—*that's* the problem.

Compulsive behavior—no matter what form it takes—is fueled and driven by inner pain. As John Bradshaw says, "The workaholic with his work, or the alcoholic with his booze, is having a love affair. Each one mood alters to avoid the feeling of loneliness and hurt. . . ."[4]

The only way to deal with the compulsion is to face up to the pain—to admit its existence to ourselves, to others, and to God. God wants to help us deal with our inner pain, but He can't do it as long as we are medicating it and pretending that it doesn't exist.

Dan understands now that, for him, work was a drug, to keep him "medicated" so that he didn't feel his pain. He hasn't yet cut back to a forty-hour work week, but he's made strides in that direction.

Tony faces an uphill struggle, but I really think he's going to win.

As far as Bill is concerned, the battle is almost over. The last time he was in my office he told me, "I feel like a big load has been taken off my back. I used to be so down on myself. I just have so much more peace in my life now."

Reflecting back on his journey toward wholeness, he said, "It was scary to look at my sadness—at first. But now I know that I don't have to put on an act for anybody anymore."

When I asked him what he had learned about his compulsive behavior, he replied, "Well, I never realized that I was doing it for a reason. I never really knew that I was afraid to let my sadness come to the surface. I didn't know it was okay to be sad."

Bill had tried to get relief from his sad feelings by overdoing everything.

"I guess it made me feel better for a while. But then I'd get really guilty and feel terrible. I was pretty depressed."

He went on. "I have a lot of sadness, which has been coming out lately. I'm realizing that I have a lot of anger, too."

"Are you still compulsive?"

"For a while, I didn't see much change in my behavior. But after a year went by, I noticed that I just wasn't doing it as much as I had before. But I've learned to give myself grace. Right now it's nowhere near as big a deal to me as it was at one time. Maybe it will always be a temptation to me, but I finally feel like I really have a choice. I can say no. And I can talk about what's really bothering me."

Bill's behavior changed because he finally chose to admit to and face up to his own pain. That was when his journey toward wholeness began.

What about you? Are you ready to allow yourself to feel as bad as you really do feel?

4
I'M JUST A HARD WORKER

Susan was about forty-five years old, attractive, and expensively dressed. She was an expressive person who used her hands as she spoke, and as they traveled through the air, I couldn't help but notice the glitter of gold, silver, and diamonds flashing from the rings on her fingers. She was also wearing the largest pearl necklace I have ever seen.

And her eyes were red from crying.

I had to wait a few moments for her to compose herself to the point where she could tell me why she had come to see me.

Finally, she spoke.

"It's my husband," she said.

There was a pause, so I urged her to continue. "What about your husband?"

"Well . . . I just can't take it anymore. He's *never* home. It's been that way for most of the eighteen years we've been married. Now that our son has gone off to college I feel completely alone." She sniffed to keep the tears from coming. "Completely, totally, alone!"

"And when he's not at home, where is he?"

"At work. Always at work. Twelve hours a day, six days a week. Sometimes more." She dabbed at her eyes with her handkerchief. "That's just not normal . . . is it?"

"Do you think it's normal?"

"Of course not!" she snorted. "It's crazy! Work has always been more important to him than family. More important than I am."

Once more, I had to wait for her composure to return.

"I don't know how many dinners got cold waiting for

33

him to come home. Finally I just stopped cooking altogether. I can't tell you how many times he's promised me that he was going to cut back. Then he took this stupid dealership over, and he's working harder than ever . . . day and night.

"He says he wants to provide for me. But I don't care about money! We have enough money! I don't want to grow old alone! I want a husband!"

What I was hearing from Susan was nothing really new. I had heard the story before from scores of women. There is a place in the wedding vows where the prospective husband is asked if he agrees to "forsake all others" and cling only to his wife. But it is not always another woman who leads a man into infidelity. It's just as likely to be his job.

Maybe we need to add another line to those wedding vows, asking the groom if he will be sure to put his wife first, even before his career. It wouldn't be a bad idea.

When it comes to the compulsive worker himself, he is rarely able to see that he has a problem. He works because he wants to be a good provider, or because he has to keep the business going, or because nobody else is really capable of doing what he does. I have never had a man come into my office and say, "You've got to help me . . . I can't seem to stop working!"

If a man who is a compulsive worker does make an appointment to see me, it's always for the same reason that was given by Dan in the last chapter. It's because his wife wanted him to come in . . . and he usually doesn't understand what all the fuss is about.

I asked Susan if her husband had always been so involved with his work. I was already pretty sure what her answer would be . . . and I wasn't surprised.

"Always. When he worked for Medical Technologies we moved seven times in ten years. He was never content . . . always trying to impress his boss. Coming in early, staying late . . . working his way up the ladder.

"At one point I begged him not to take the next promotion. He was already making enough money so that we were comfortable, and I didn't want to pull up stakes and move again."

She told me how he had even been transferred to To-kyo for a while. She had hated the year or so they had lived there, feeling totally cut off from her family and friends in the United States.

Before she left my office, she told me that she really wanted me to talk to her husband. She had gone so far as to make an appointment for him, which he agreed to keep.

He was right on schedule, a couple of days later.

When I probed him about his tendency to spend too much time at work, he just shrugged.

"Yes, I know there's a problem," he admitted. "But I don't know if I can do anything about it. I'm not sure I can change."

And, like most men with this compulsion, John wasn't really sure he *wanted* to change.

This type of lifestyle is especially dangerous for the Christian man, who sees hard work as a virtue. And, who believes, therefore, that the harder you work, the more virtuous you are.

Anything that usurps God's rightful place as the top priority of your life is an idol.

The problem of work compulsion is often found among the professional clergy themselves, who sometimes become so busy *serving* God that they have very little time left for getting to know Him . . . or for spending time *with* Him. Many pastors, youth workers, elders, missionaries, dea-cons, and Sunday school teachers could undoubtedly be considered to be workaholics.

For example, there is Pastor Bob.

Pastor Bob tries to fix everyone and everything. He seems to feel personally responsible if there is anyone within a fifty-mile radius who is hurting. He is involved with every detail of the church, from photocopying the program to picking out the hymns for the Sunday morning worship service.

Actually, the services at his church could be described more as one-man shows than as worship services. Taking a look at Pastor Bob's daily calendar would weaken the knees of the strongest man. It starts at 6:30 A.M. with prayer in the church sanctuary. At that time of morning his kids are just getting out of bed, so he doesn't have a chance to eat with them before they go to school. In fact, his wife is usually still asleep when he first leaves the house in the morning, although he'll go over and give her a quick kiss on the cheek . . . when he remembers.

The morning portion of his calendar is filled with meetings, Bible studies—different groups for different days of the week—followed by lunch with one of his assistants or an elder or trustee of the church. (He stops for lunch because a man *has* to eat, but he figures he can still use that time to discuss church business.)

His afternoon calendar is just as full as the morning, with counseling appointments, meetings, and other church activities.

It seems that there is some sort of committee or board meeting every night, and it is rare that he gets home before his wife and children are in bed.

This type of schedule continues all week. And then, of course, Sunday is Pastor Bob's big day.

By the time the Sunday evening service is over, he has gone through six full days without spending any meaningful time with his family. Come to think of it, he hasn't *really* spent much time with the Lord . . . in prayer, or just waiting on the Lord, seeking His direction. If the Lord did speak, He would have to speak loudly to get through all the noise and confusion in Pastor Bob's mind.

Because he wants to do everything by himself, he is doing a lot of things he really shouldn't have to do. For example, he is counseling people that really ought to be referred to professional Christian help. He is involved in the smallest details of church life—details that are irrelevant to the exercise of his ministry. He would be shocked and hurt if he knew how the members of his staff felt about him. They feel overworked and misunderstood, and one or two of them have taken to doing unflattering impersonations of him behind his back.

Saddest of all, his flock isn't even being fed. If he spent half as much time developing his sermons as he does on clerical and administrative details, his sermons could provide some spiritual nourishment.

The end result of all of this is that he's never worked harder in his life—but he's never been less effective.

I've spent quite a bit of time talking about Pastor Bob. I realize this. But that's because I have seen him so many times, in so many "men of the cloth." Sometimes they end up destroying themselves, and their marriages. They wind up with children who don't know them . . . or don't even *want* to know them, and who turn their backs on the church (and the Lord) because they feel that it was the church that deprived them of their father while they were growing up.

Saddest of all, a man like Pastor Bob may get to the point where he totally burns out, and realizes that he's even forgotten what all the work was for in the first place.

A compulsion toward work is never, ever beneficial. The end result is always tragedy in one form or another. This sort of behavior is not what God wants. It is not what He blesses. It is certainly not what He expects from those He has called into His service.

A Matter of Motive

The compulsive worker doesn't put in long hours because he *has* to, but because he *wants* to. He is the man who chooses to spend time on the job *instead* of being with his family. He uses his work as a drug, because he's afraid to face up to the pain in his life. His work medicates him so that he doesn't have to feel a thing.

There are six particular symptoms that are exhibited by the compulsive worker as follows:

1. He is critical of others.
2. He has a need to control.
3. He desires position and recognition.
4. He is out of touch with his feelings.
5. He is physically restless.
6. He is angry.
7. He is insecure.

We're going to take a look at these aspects of the compulsive worker's personality, one at a time. Before we do, though, I want to remind you that these are *general* characteristics. Not every compulsive worker demonstrates all of these character traits. But you will find several of them in every work-obsessed male. Let's examine each one.

He is critical of others. Actually, it's not only others who feel the sting of his critical nature. He's very tough on himself, too.

Mistakes, whether made by others or by himself, tend to make this man angry because he wants things to be perfect. He will often tell you that he works as hard as he does because he can't get anybody else to do things "right." What he probably means by this is that he can't get anyone to do things the way he thinks they ought to be done. Because of this, he often has trouble delegating authority, and tends to see himself as indispensable.

He has a need to control. As I mentioned earlier, the compulsive worker has a difficult time delegating work because he is so critical. Nobody can do it—whatever it is—up to his exacting standards. Sometimes he's not even sure how he wants it done, so he can't explain it to anyone else. He's likely to say something like, "I may not know what I want, but I'll know what I like when I see it."

Well, the truth may be that he's not going to like much of anything unless he does it himself.

Do you see within yourself the need to control? If so, where did it come from? There are several reasons why people tend to develop controlling personalities, but three in particular stand out.

- A controlling personality may be the result of a person's position in the family when he was growing up, or the expectations his parents had for him. Most often, this is the first-born child, who has greater pressure placed on him because of his place in the family. Whether or not he is the first born, he is still the child who, for whatever reason, was always expected to "take charge," and "be a good example" for his younger brothers or sisters, and who was always asked to be "the man of the house" when his father was away. Because of this, he is likely to grow up with the attitude that he's got to be in charge. He may not like this position, but it's just the way it is . . . and he *does* feel like the world is sitting on his shoulders.

- A controlling attitude may also develop in someone who has suffered some great loss in life—whether that loss is real or perceived. Whatever happened to hurt him, he wants to do everything within his power to make sure it doesn't happen again, and the only way he can do that is if he keeps things under control.

- A third reason why a controlling attitude may take shape in someone's life is that he has lived for years with a situation he *can't* control. For example, a boy may grow up in a family where his mother and father fight all of the time. He can't do anything to stop their fighting and he knows it. It's totally beyond his control. As a result, he demands complete control over other areas of his life. Whatever he can control, he will control.

Have you noticed the common denominator in all of these situations? In each, the man's compulsive need to control has come about because of need, loss, or pain in his life. Often, that need or loss is buried so deeply that the victim would likely deny that it even exists. He may not be consciously aware of its presence. But it's there, just the same . . . and it's causing tremendous problems.

In the first example, it is the pain of undue pressure brought to bear on him by his parents. In the second situation, it is the pain of loss. And, in the third instance, the need to control is a reaction against unpleasant things that were beyond his control.

If you see yourself in any of these situations, you need to know that the only way you can overcome your need to exercise control is to face up to the pain and the need in your life.

He needs position and recognition. Some people go crazy

if they don't have a ladder to climb.

That's what was going on with Susan's husband, John, who fought hard to get every promotion his company had to give. Long after he had it made, after he was making more than enough money to keep his family living in comfort, he was still scrambling like a rookie trying to make it up the first few rungs of the ladder.

Others run at ninety miles an hour all of the time not because they're trying to *climb* the ladder, but because they're desperately trying to stay right where they are. They may not be going up the ladder, but they certainly don't want to go down the ladder, either. This person thinks that if he doesn't scrap and scrape and scramble for everything he's worth, he's going to lose his place. He'll simply be passed by, and one of the "young turks" will soon be moving into his office.

Again, a compulsion toward work does not have as much to do with the hours a person is working as it does with his motivation for working them. For example, the work-compulsive pastor can have dozens of assistants to help him, and he'll still be running ragged trying to do everything himself. That's just the way he is.

He is out of touch with his feelings. The compulsive worker, like all true compulsives, finds it difficult to identify and express his emotions. Even if he feels passionately about something, chances are that he doesn't want to talk about it. Instead, he channels his passion and energy into his work.

It's not uncommon for the wife of a such a man to tell me, "He works all day, and then when he comes home he doesn't have anything to say to me. The least he could do would be to talk to me about things."

The reason this person has trouble expressing his feelings is that to do so would be facing up to the pain and loss he has inside, and chances are very good that he has a lot of pain. You see, if he goes mucking around down in his true feelings and emotions, all that pain is likely to come floating to the surface where he'll have to deal with it, and he doesn't want that to happen.

Now, the compulsive worker who has trouble expressing himself may read that last paragraph and say, "What pain? I don't have any pain." Yes, he does, but he has pushed it down so deep that his conscious mind doesn't even know it's there. Yet anyone around him who is sensitive will testify that they can feel the strong emotions emitting from him.

He might even be to the point where he knows what it was that originally caused him such pain, but feels that he got over whatever it was a long time ago. But, really, he's not over it. He never dealt with it at all.

Perhaps he has been caught up in work-related performance for so long that he's forgotten the sense of inadequacy and pain that originally compelled him to strive so hard to achieve.

He is physically restless. A compulsive worker tends to be jittery. He may be uncomfortable just sitting around relaxing. He feels as if he *always* has to be doing something.

You would think that because of his boundless energy, this person would be a "ball of fire" on the job, getting more done than anyone else. Unfortunately, the opposite is often true. He can actually be less efficient than other workers because of his inability to delegate work, and his tendency to want to do everything himself. And his work-centered lifestyle is not likely to make him the most popular or appreciated guy on the job.

Like other compulsive types, this type of man is hard to work with, and even harder to live with.

He is angry. Many compulsive workers are intrinsically hostile and angry men. Work becomes a socially acceptable manner in which to discharge the aggression and anger they feel.

Where does this anger and rage come from? Perhaps from a deprived childhood, which causes this man to shake his fist at the world and say, "I'll never be poor like my dad was!" Or perhaps his anger comes from bad experiences in junior high school, when teachers ridiculed him and put him down in front of his peers for his inability to do well in English or math. It could come from anywhere, and he is the only one who has the ability to uncover the source of his anger and to deal with it.

It would be even better if he could face up to the source of his anger—his inner pain—and deal with it once and for all.

He is insecure. More than once I have asked a compulsive worker why he works so hard and received this answer:

"Because I have to work while I can. The work might not be there tomorrow."

I especially hear this kind of talk from men who are in business for themselves. They fear that the economy might get worse, or that competition will take their business away, or that things are just going to change in some undefinable way so that the services they offer are no longer needed.

The man who thinks this way is terribly insecure. He's killing himself today, and destroying his family relationships, because he's afraid the "well" is going to dry up, that there won't be anything for him to do tomorrow, and he and his family are likely to wind up in the poor house.

Actually, there is a deeper problem than insecurity. The real difficulty is that this man is trusting in the work he has to do, rather than in the Lord, who has *provided* the work. He is demonstrating by his insecure behavior that he doesn't really believe he can trust God to provide for him tomorrow.

Are You a Compulsive Worker?

As I've said before, most compulsive workers don't see themselves for what they are. They believe they are all-around good people who just happen to be hard workers. What about you? Are you compulsive when it comes to work? Or does someone you know (and perhaps even live with) fall into this category?

How do you know if you are a compulsive worker? Take this little quiz and see.

Answer yes or no to the following questions:

_____ Do you feel uncomfortable on vacations?

_____ Would you rather be at work than anywhere else?

_____ Do you feel guilty when you're not working?

_____ Has your spouse ever expressed concern to you about your work-related absences from home?

_____ Deep down, do you feel that if you want something done right, you have to do it yourself?

_____ Do you spend more than eight or nine hours a day at work away from your family? And do you work on weekends?

_____ Do you work when you really could be resting or relaxing?

_____ Is your *Daytimer* or your *Franklin Planner* the most important book you own? Do you take it with you everywhere you go?

If you answered yes to any one of the questions, you may be compulsive in relation to your job. If you answered yes to two or more of the questions, then you are a compulsive worker.

Work as a Drug

For some men, work can be as strong as cocaine in its ability to bring on a rush and to alter the mood.

The man who uses work in this way has many inner struggles. Primarily, he feels insignificant. Work has become a way for him to attain a positive identity.

He avoids emotional intimacy because this would make him vulnerable, and that's the last thing he would ever want to be. This may be part of the reason he spends so much time away from his wife and family. He may really love his wife, but he just doesn't know how to relate to her on a truly open, intimate level, and he never feels that more keenly than when he's with her. And so, to escape his feeling of failure in that area of his life, he throws himself into his work.

That's where he knows he can succeed. But sadly, even there, he is only briefly satisfied with his latest achievement.

He seldom takes the time to stop and bask in the glory of what he has accomplished, because there is always another mountain waiting on the horizon.

Work can be so addicting to this man that he actually experiences withdrawal symptoms when he's away from it. On a day when he's not at the office, a Sunday perhaps, he may experience withdrawal symptoms such as depression, restlessness, and despair. He may crave sweets because he needs an extra boost on that day, or he may drink to excess.

The idea of "work as a drug" can especially be seen in the behavior of the businessman who seeks the exhilaration that comes from making "the big deal." He gets a high out of wheeling and dealing that no druggie ever dreamed of.

In the popular movie, *Wall Street,* Michael Douglas portrayed this type of person. Douglas's performance as Gordon Gecko was a perfect example of the competitive, cut-throat, compulsive worker who lives for the thrill of the "big score."

Some Differences Between Hard Work and Compulsion

Even though we've spent quite a bit of time talking about the characteristics of a work-related compulsion, there are still likely to be some questions as to just when a man's dedication to his job becomes compulsive.

There are some obvious differences between the compulsive worker and the ordinary Christian man who just works hard, especially with regard to the following areas:

Ambition
Identity
Family life
Control

Let's take a brief look at the different approaches to these four areas of life:

AMBITION

HARD WORKER:

Ambition is a good thing if it is kept in check—surrendered to God, and not allowed to become the controlling force in a person's life. The best attitude is the one that says, "I want to do and be my best, but I am willing to follow the Lord's leading for my career." This person is at peace, whatever he is doing, as long as he knows he is in God's will.

COMPULSIVE WORKER:

In the compulsive worker, "ambition" is nothing more than a cloak to disguise restless dissatisfaction with what one has already achieved. It is a striving for more, rooted in dissatisfaction and a lack of serenity. The compulsive worker always thinks, "If only I could make more, do more, achieve more ... if I could get more money, more prestige, more power, and become less dependent upon others." Sadly, he will never, ever be able to achieve those goals, and thus become satisfied with himself and what he has done.

IDENTITY

HARD WORKER:

His identity is quite separate and apart from his work. He can detach himself from his work role and still maintain the integrity of his being. This is expressed by his ability to set boundaries around his work. Generally, he draws his self-worth from his understanding of himself as someone created in the image and likeness of God.

COMPULSIVE WORKER:

The compulsive worker's sense of self is dependent upon his performance on the job. His identity is not rooted in "being," but rather in "doing." He thinks that his self-worth depends upon the things he has accomplished, but, sadly, he's never likely to accomplish enough that he can feel good about himself.

FAMILY LIFE

HARD WORKER:

The normal man, who is simply a hard worker, works out of a sense of vocation, duty, service, and obligation to provide a reasonable level of material security for his family. "Reasonable level" may be left to his conscience, along with

COMPULSIVE WORKER:

The compulsive worker generally doesn't have much of a family life. He may tell you that he's doing what he's doing for the sake of his family. He may even believe it himself. But a close look at the situation will show you immediately the guidance and accountability that may come from a relationship with an older, more mature believer. This worker makes sure that his job is not coming between him and his family.

that it just isn't so. He regularly works more than eight or nine hours per day, more than five days per week. When he does get home "on time," he invariably has brought several hours' worth of work with him. His relationships with the members of his family definitely take a backseat to his career.

CONTROL

HARD WORKER:

The normal hard worker is in control of his career. He purposes to be yielded to God.

COMPULSIVE WORKER:

The compulsive hard worker's career is in control of him. Otherwise, he is yielded to no one.

Dick was recovering from his first heart attack at the age of forty-eight. His high-pressure, fast-paced, work-centered lifestyle had finally caught up with him; in fact, it had almost dealt him a death blow.

"I could have died," he told me. "It's really a miracle that I'm alive. My heart attack really caught my attention."

"And what have you learned?" I asked.

"Well . . . when I was in the hospital, unable to work . . . I didn't have anything else to do but lie there and think about things. And when I did, everything just kind of caught up with me. I realized that I was really unhappy. Unhappy with my life. Unhappy with my marriage. And with myself."

He began to weep quietly, and it took a few moments before he was able to continue.

Then he said, "I've been carrying around a grief and rage so powerful it's unreal. As a kid, I never had time to stop and lick my wounds. I was too busy surviving."

Dick explained that his father had been a heavy drinker, who never did anything with his children. Dick remembered how he would wake up at night and hear his drunken father loudly carrying on.

"I had forgotten how scared I used to be at night. I was so insecure and frightened. It seems like these old memories, these old pains are coming back. I really don't know what to do with all of these feelings. It hurts so much . . . and I'm so angry!"

I nodded in understanding, and he continued.

"I've been carrying around this big thing in my chest. I've been so busy that I haven't even stopped to realize how angry I am. In fact . . . I think I'm furious!"

His voice trailed off and then he began to cry again, softly at first, and then louder, until he was crying tears that should have been wept years ago.

I said, "Your tears are the healthiest thing about you."

I knew he was beginning to move toward healing.

5
SEX DRIVE OR OVERDRIVE?

Christian men simply aren't supposed to have sexual compulsions. But they do.

Part of the problem for the Christian man who has a particular weakness in this area is that he simply can't escape sexually explicit images and "come-ons" no matter what he does.

In other words, sex sells, and the world has no qualms at all about using it.

It is very difficult for the average American male to get through his average American day without being bombarded by a number of sexually explicit images or messages. If he stops by the magazine stand to pick up a copy of *Time* or *Newsweek,* female flesh will be enticing him from every direction. There's cleavage on the cover of *Cosmo,* the swimsuit issue of *Sports Illustrated* and other shapely women in various stages of undress looking out from the covers of several other periodicals—not to mention *Playboy* and the like. And let that same man flip through his ordinary news magazine or a newspaper, and even there he's going to be hit with a number of sexual images—and they're not necessarily selling lingerie either. It almost seems sometimes that if an advertiser can think of a way to use sex to sell his product, then he's going to do it—no matter how unrelated to sex his product might be.

Next, this average guy walks past a movie theater, and the posters for the movies that are now playing are likely to continue this sexual assault on his masculine senses. Most every movie with a rating higher than G has some sexual content these days.

And most of the shows on television are heading in that direction. (If you want a real education into how sexual today's television programs have become, sit through one or two afternoons of soap operas.) But if you think the shows on TV are bombarding you with sexual images, just wait until you see the commercials—especially the ones for beer, perfume, or clothes. And then, if he happens to be changing channels and flips past MTV, watch out . . . because record companies have apparently discovered that explicitly sexy videos are a great way to help sell mediocre (or worse) music.

My point is that you would have to wear blinders to avoid seeing at least some of the sexual images that come at you from all sides. No wonder so many Christian men have such a struggle with the sexual aspect of their natures.

Many good men have been seduced by the sexual temptations that are thrown at them in this way every day. Young men are especially vulnerable—teenagers and those in their twenties and thirties.

JOHN

For example, I think of a young man named John who came to me seeking help. John's marriage had almost been destroyed by his sexual compulsion, and he was desperate in his desire to save it. He truly loved his wife and wanted to please her, just as he wanted to be truly pleasing to God, but his preoccupation with sex was so great that he knew he couldn't overcome it on his own.

Early in his teen years, aroused by the sexual images that constantly came at him through the media, and that piqued his curiosity, John became involved in pornography. When he looked at the sexy photos of beautiful women, or watched the raunchy videos, he felt a sense of excitement and power. He could escape the pain of his daily existence—his loneliness, uncertainty about the future, and feelings of awkwardness and emptiness—the sorts of feelings that almost all teenage boys experience at one time or another. It was as if the women in the videos were performing for him and him alone, and that made him feel like a "cool dude."

When John first started looking at pornography, he would only occasionally "sneak a peek" at a sexually explicit magazine or rent a racy video. But like all compulsions, this one drew him in deeper and deeper.

But then John became a Christian. He told the Lord that he was willing to surrender every aspect of his life, and he meant it. John just knew that his compulsive interest in pornography had been washed away by the blood of Christ. And for a while, that's how it seemed to be.

But his "victory" was only a temporary one, and after a while he was as deeply into his compulsion as ever. And now that he was a Christian, and knew that what he was doing was wrong, he desperately wanted to stop—but couldn't. He felt like a hypocrite because the life he was living wasn't the same as the image he was presenting to his Christian friends. He felt worthless, like the worst sinner who ever lived. He was caught in a "cycle of shame" that is typical of the compulsive person.

"Addicts go from one extreme to another in alternating rhythms. . . . They try to reach the impossible norms of their parents, family, and culture. But the feelings, needs, and drives they have been taught to ignore keep reasserting themselves. As with a dam no longer able to contain the floodwaters, there is a collapse and none of the waters are held."[1]

Along the way, John met and married a lovely young Christian woman.

Unfortunately, by that time his sexuality was extremely dysfunctional. He viewed sex as a quick "high" that made him feel good temporarily—made him forget his pain. He was unable to experience true intimacy with his wife, and didn't really try to please her in bed, as long as he was getting what *he* wanted. Sex to him was not a beautiful, mutual sharing between husband and wife, but rather an egocentric attempt to discharge emotional and physical tension.

His wife complained about him not "being there emotionally" for her. She described him as being like a brick wall, unfeeling and aloof.

What she didn't understand was that John really did love her very much. He just didn't know how to express his love for her in a physical way. Men who are like John really don't know what it means to "make love" to their wives. They "have sex." And there is a tremendous difference between those two activities.

Many men do exactly what John was doing—they use sex as a means of relief, of medicating unpleasant feelings. And if they medicate themselves over a long period, they may stop feeling altogether.

John was fortunate. He became engaged in the journey toward spiritual wholeness as outlined throughout this book, and he has now had four years of victory in this area of his life. His marriage is in good shape, and he spends some of his time working with others who are trying to overcome compulsive behavior with regard to sex or pornography.

John has successfully overcome his compulsion primarily because he knew that he had a serious problem, and he was willing to take whatever steps were necessary to overcome it. Through counseling, he came to realize that the biggest problem in his life was himself, and his inability to accept life on life's own terms—to face up to and deal with his inner pain and need, and the insecurities he felt. Once he realized this and stopped denying his problem, his recovery was certain. Not immediate . . . but certain. He was able to deal with his compulsive behavior before it completely gained control of him; before it became an addiction.

PHIL

Phil wasn't so fortunate.

He was an elder in a small church, who had been married for eight years. And like John, he was living a "Jekyll and Hyde" kind of life, presenting one image to his Christian acquaintances, and another to the world. Phil had started out on the road to sexual addiction in the same way John had done—with occasional visits to adult bookstores or triple-x-rated movies.

But instead of seeking the help he needed, he had gone deeper and deeper into his compulsive behavior to the point where he could not seem to extricate himself.

Every few months he would go into a nearby town where he would visit a massage parlor. There, for $75 an hour, he would engage in sex with a prostitute. He enjoyed variety in his compulsivity, so he moved around from establishment to establishment, rarely having the same woman twice. He would go on a binge every three months or so.

Afterward, he would become almost suicidal with guilt. Yet despite all of his guilt, deep sorrow, and resolve that he wasn't ever going to do it again, he would never get through more than a few months without falling again. And when he did, he hated himself for it.

Phil would often fast and pray for deliverance, vowing to God that he would never sin in this manner again. He saw his problem as being purely spiritual. If he could just repent harder and forsake his sin, he would be okay.

On occasion, he was called on to deliver a sermon in the church where he was an elder, and he often preached on the subject of godly repentance. If anyone had known what was really going on in Phil's life, they would have noticed that after one of his encounters, he always preached with extraordinary zeal and anger against the sins of the flesh.

As often happens, Phil's wife called to find out about the possibility of marriage counseling. She loved her husband, but found him to be increasingly distant and emotionally cold. She described living with him like "living with a computer in a perpetual bad mood!" I had to smile over her description, but after our first meeting, I understood exactly what she was talking about. The "computer-with-a-bad-mood" analogy fit him to a tee.

After one visit with the two of them together, I suggested that he come and see me alone. I thought that maybe he would be more open with me if there were only the two of us in the room. I was wrong.

He was extremely difficult to communicate with, but I

did manage to find out a few things about him. He had grown up in a home that was tyrannized by an alcoholic father. He had no real close male friends, and even though he paid lip service to his superiors in the church, he was really accountable to no one. Because of his relationship with his father, he was openly distrustful of any male authority figure. And because he could not see that there were emotional and psychological aspects of his behavior, he was a poor candidate for change. As far as he was concerned, the only problems he had were spiritual in nature, and that's how he was going to deal with them.

I sensed that he was a deeply sad man, and in many ways he reminded me of a little boy. He was also very angry, and even though most of his anger was directed at himself, there was enough left over for a few other people, including me. I knew that the only reason he came to see me was as a gesture of good will toward his wife, and he seemed totally unwilling to share his inner thoughts and feelings.

Most of the time, all he wanted to do was talk abstractly and intellectually about theological issues. I sensed that he was trying to understand himself from a purely theological viewpoint in a rather detached manner.

I was also pretty sure he was trying to test me to see if I was evangelical and biblically sound. For example, he wanted to know my views on sanctification and holiness.

"Don't you agree that all sin is a result of willful disobedience? Don't you agree that Christians don't have to sin if they really turn from it?"

"Yes," I agreed, "sin is willful disobedience. But sometimes the will itself is sin-sick."

He wasn't about to accept that.

"But doesn't the Word applied to the heart through the power of the Holy Spirit enable the believer to have victory over sin?"

"That's true. But maybe some sins are harder to quit than others. And maybe some sins take longer to overcome—and until the victory has arrived we need to depend on His grace."

He seemed to think about it for a moment . . . but then

dismissed me with an impatient wave of his hand. "The Bible is all we need!"

I wasn't surprised when I didn't hear from him for a few weeks after that. But then he called to say he needed to see me right away. I scheduled an appointment for the following day.

When he arrived, he seemed more subdued than I had ever seen him. He entered my office, shook my hand, and sat down with an air of resignation.

Finally, he was ready to talk.

"I saw a prostitute last weekend."

I nodded, and he continued.

"The fact is that I've been going to massage parlors for years," he said, with more than a hint of sorrow in his voice. "You know . . . I really want to stop. I don't know why I keep going back. I'm fine for a while, and then I lose my temper over something stupid . . . and I go out and find a prostitute."

"How do you feel right before you see her?" I asked.

"Excited. My heart pounds."

"How do you feel during your time with her?"

"Like a million bucks."

"Afterwards?"

"Oh . . . horrible! Depressed. I hate myself so much that I really feel like dying. But then I turn around and do the same thing again!"

"It sounds to me as if the whole experience is like a drug," I exclaimed. "You sound just like some of the alcoholics who come for counsel."

"Well . . . I'm going to try harder to stop."

"I think you need to surrender . . . not try harder. If you do try harder and succeed, it may give you a false sense of security. Unless you deal with the underlying emotions that fuel your compulsion, you may eventually go back to it."

He let out a big sigh, as if he was exasperated by my thick-headedness.

"I told you . . . I don't believe in psychology. I believe in miracles. I think God can heal me outright. Don't you?

I thought this was a *Christian* counseling center!"

"Yes . . ." I insisted, "I believe in miracles, too. And I think it's a miracle that you came to see me, considering how you feel about psychology!"

We both laughed about that.

Phil agreed that he would come back for a few more sessions. But he was never really able to see that his problem was emotional and psychological *as well* as spiritual. He could not overcome his belief in the Just-Do-It Approach, which, as you may remember from chapter 1, says that if a person will only pray more, read the Bible more, and perhaps fast more, he's going to be able to overcome any sinful compulsion.

Phil felt that he was a very weak person because he could not overcome his sexual addiction, and he *hated* weak people.

Poor Phil eventually quit coming to see me—but it was really just as well, because we weren't getting anywhere. And then he got sloppy. Instead of paying for his "high" with cash, as was his custom; in a frenzy of compulsivity he wrote a check. When his wife went through their bank statement and saw a $75 check made out to "Yvonne's Escort Service," she threatened to leave him.

Of course, Phil begged her for another chance. He was going to change, she'd see. Only he couldn't change. Finally, his wife had had enough, and filed for divorce. Through it all, Phil continued to frequent massage parlors. He also refused to quit preaching—thundering from the pulpit about the dangers of the sins of the flesh—somehow hoping that the fervor of his own voice could set him free. As far as I know, he's still out there, visiting massage parlors and doing who knows what else. And probably still thinking that if he can only try harder he'll be all right. He probably still hates himself.

I feel certain he could be free today if only he had been willing to face up to the truth of his sexual compulsivity, and the underlying causes of that compulsive behavior.

Unfortunately, he could not bear to admit his addiction—that his habit was like a drug—a drug from which he could not free himself.

How About You?

Phil was obviously compulsive sexually, but what about the average Christian man today? Is he sexually compulsive at times? The question really is, how about you?

Perhaps you cannot relate to the man who would visit a prostitute, or to a guy like Bill, the man we met in the first chapter, who was having difficulty dealing with compulsive masturbation. But then again, maybe you find yourself checking out the attractive women in church when you know you should be listening to the sermon. Maybe your eyes just automatically follow the contours of a shapely woman's body as she walks by.

It could be that you find yourself drawn to provocative material on cable television when you are away from home on a business trip—or that you keep a stack of "girlie" magazines in the bottom drawer of your nightstand.

Respecting Yourself

There are many reasons why men can get "out of control" sexually, but what it all boils down to here—as with the other compulsions we've discussed—is that sex is being used to make them feel better . . . temporarily.

The sexually compulsive man doesn't see sexual love for what it is—a means of loving communication between one man and one woman who have given their lives to each other. He sees sex as a means of demonstrating his power. Through sex, he can conquer, dominate, be in control.

For that reason, the sexually compulsive male will often tend to dwell on aggressive or degrading sexual fantasies—perhaps fantasies about punishing some woman, using her in some way, or being idolized by her.

The sexually compulsive husband is likely to disregard his wife's pleas for intimacy and deeper communication. He considers trivial her desire for gentleness and more time in their sexual encounter.

In reality, there are some men who have "had sex" with dozens of women, but who have never "made love" to a woman in their lives. They don't know how to be intimate with another, when they have been hiding such a large part of themselves for so long.

"Falling"

Most of us are shocked whenever we read of a prominent person getting caught in a sex scandal. The tendency is to think something like, "Wow, I didn't realize what a sleaze that guy was." Or we may think, "I can't believe that guy would risk everything—his wife, his children, his career—for a few moments of sexual pleasure!" What we don't understand when we make statements like that is that sexual compulsion can be just as strong as any other compulsion.

When a man decides to go to a "fat farm" to lose weight, and to get a grip on his compulsive eating, people generally applaud. When a workaholic decides to cut back his hours so he can devote more time to his family, he is praised. But when a sexually compulsive man tries to get help, he is often made to feel ashamed for having this problem in the first place.

In his book *Don't Call It Love,* Patrick Carnes lists some of the severe consequences of sexual compulsivity.[2]
Among them:

- Many sexually compulsive people talk of near-death experiences from accidents, violence, high-risk situations, or rape.
- Such people recognize AIDS as perhaps the most lethal complication to their illness.
- Many of them have lost a partner or spouse (40 percent) due to their behavior, and most have experienced severe marital or relationship problems (70 percent).
- Some of them have lost rights to their children (13 percent), and some have found it necessary to cut their ties with their family of origin (8 percent).
- For a majority, sexual compulsion has had severe financial consequences (58 percent).
- Some of them reported losing the opportunity to

work in the career of their choice (27 percent).

Obviously, sexually compulsive behavior has a high price tag for anyone, but the price can be even higher for the sexually compulsive man who is trying, but failing, to live the Christian life.

A Heaping Helping of Guilt and Shame

The shame and guilt that society in general and the church in particular piles upon the heads of such men is surpassed only by the shame and guilt they themselves feel.

For example, I remember a young man named Mark.

Mark immediately noticed the attractive young secretary that had been hired to work in his office. He found himself sucking in his gut whenever he needed to ask her a question or get her to do some work for him. He'd also put on his best smile, say a few witty things, and do his best to leave her laughing. Once, when she bent over to get something out of the files for him, he found himself looking down her blouse.

He tried to tell himself that it had just been an accident. He hadn't *meant* to look at her that way. But really, he knew he'd done it on purpose, and he hoped she hadn't noticed. What would she think if she knew? What would the people at church say? He felt that he'd disappointed the Lord. He was sure his wife would "kill" him if she ever caught him looking at another woman like that.

And then one night a few days later, while making love to his wife, Mark began to fantasize that he was making love to the new secretary instead. The fantasy lasted for quite a long time before he realized what he was doing. And then, he felt terrible.

But for Mark, trying *not* to fantasize only made it worse. It was like the old challenge, "Don't think about pink elephants for the next five minutes." The more he tried not to fantasize, the more he did fantasize, and the more upset with himself, and the more overwhelmed with guilt, he became.

He hadn't slept with the secretary. But the way he felt

about it, he might as well have.

Tim's story was a little bit different. He was on a business trip, staying all alone in a hotel, when he noticed that for a few dollars extra he could see an "adult" movie on the TV in his room. His curiosity overtook him and he punched the necessary buttons and sat back for a look. As he watched, his heart began to beat faster and faster. He was more than interested in what was going on that screen. He was excited by it. Turned on. And he was hooked.

He was also nearly destroyed by his feelings of guilt and shame.

Are Sexual Sins Really the Worst Sins?

One of the difficulties in helping Christian men overcome sexual compulsivity is, frankly, that the church has tended to foster the unhealthy notion that sexual sins are somehow worse than other kinds of sins.

This notion comes primarily from 1 Corinthians 6:18, where the apostle Paul writes: "Flee from sexual immorality. All other sins a man commits are outside his body, but he who sins sexually sins against his own body." But even here, Paul is not really saying that sex sins are worse, that they can't be forgiven, or that God is going to exact a special kind of vengeance upon those who commit them. What he's saying is that if you commit a sin that is against your own body, you are very likely going to have to pay the consequences—and we're certainly seeing the truth of that statement in our day, since AIDs and other sexually transmitted diseases are rampant throughout the world.

Sin is sin, whether we're talking about envy, slothfulness, stealing, murder, or sexual impurity—and all sin can be washed away by the blood of Christ.

The truth is that most men wrestle with their sexuality at some point in their lives. The aggressive nature of the male sex drive can be difficult to tame. Biologically, men have the hormone testosterone in their bloodstream, which causes them to initiate sexual relations. The world would be an empty place, population-wise, if it were not for this powerful hormone.

Back in chapter 1, I talked briefly about the aggressive nature of the male sex drive. Men don't need to be shamed for having a sex drive. Many women cannot understand the almost "mechanical" nature of this drive. On the other hand they become angry or berate their husbands when they feel belittled or made to feel like an object. Men need to learn how to be affectionate without immediately going into sexual high-gear.

Every Christian ought to realize that sex, the way God intended it, is very good. It's not only the way by which new life is brought into the world, but it is the means through which a man and woman are able to communicate on the deepest possible level. However, as can happen with all of the good things God has created for our pleasure, the compulsive type will often overdo it with sex until all control is lost and the compulsion takes over. For the truly sexually compulsive, his sexuality becomes a source of great conflict.

Patrick Carnes writes, "Only an out-of-control pattern along with other classic signs of addiction—obsession, powerlessness, and use of sex as a means to relieve pain—indicate the presence of sexual addiction."[3]

He says there are at least six ways in which compulsive sexual behavior deviates from the norm:

1. It involves exploitation of others.
2. It is not likely to be based on or result in intimacy.
3. Women are looked upon as objects of sexual gratification, rather than as human beings.
4. There is great dissatisfaction, brought on partly by the fact that sexual pleasure is only a temporary anesthetic for the person's pain and not a cure.
5. The behaviors create shame and secrecy.
6. There is a direct correlation between sexual excitement and fear.

Peter Trachtenberg has talked with hundreds of sexually compulsive men, and he says that he found "an underlying hunger and impoverishment of spirit, and an unconscious view of women as faceless instruments of

pleasure, ego gratification, and relief. All women are in-
terchangeable," he writes, "and divided into two rigid cat-
egories: those to pursue and those to run from."[4]

He adds that, for many men, "promiscuity is not a chase
after pleasure, but a flight from pain and fear."[5]

Check Your Attitude About Sex

Having said that most men, Christians included, have
a strong sex drive, I hasten to add that the Christian must
be very careful that his sexual impulses aren't just floating
free—focusing on any attractive woman who happens to
pass by. They should be focused on the woman who is his
life's partner: his wife.

It is sometimes difficult, because of the powerful nature
of the male sex drive, to distinguish between behavior that
is compulsive, and behavior that is merely improper or ill-
advised. But the following are a few questions designed to
check your attitude about sex. They are intended to pro-
voke thought, so you can see if there are areas where you
need to change:

- When an attractive woman walks by, do you find
  yourself wondering what it would be like to have sex
  with her, or what she would look like without her
  clothes on?
- Do you fantasize about other women while you are
  making love to your wife?
- Do you have difficulty relating to a woman as a human being?
- Do you find yourself "checking out" other women's
  bodies?
- Do you read pornographic magazines?
- Do you watch pornographic videos?
- Do you masturbate? Frequently?

If your honest answer to one or more of these questions
is yes, then you are likely to have a sexual compulsion.

The Problem With Masturbation

Like other counselors, I am often asked if masturbation in and of itself is a sin.

Opinions among well-meaning Christians are certainly wide-ranging, with some vehemently condemning it and others seeing it as a God-given "safety valve" to help prevent fornication or adultery. But where does the truth lie?

In that there is no discussion of masturbation in the Bible, perhaps the real question should be, "*When* is masturbation sinful?" I believe that, like many other issues of spirituality, behavior, and the Christian faith, this is a question to be answered by the personal conscience and convictions of the individual involved. Because of the confusion that surrounds this issue, the person may want to discuss this with his counselor or pastor.

Some Christian conselors feel that for an adolescent who may have ten or more years of sexual maturity before he is able to marry, masturbation can be a safe outlet for sexual tension. Their perspective is that the suppression of the urge to masturbate, especially in a young person, can be unhealthy, and the urge to stop can become so obsessive that it turns attention on the activity and away from Christ's grace.

Some counselors also feel that masturbation might be appropriate when one's spouse is unavailable for some reason over a long period of time. After all, they say, a man who is "spent" sexually is much less likely to become involved in an affair.

But a word of warning is in order here: masturbation can become obsessive and compulsive. And, where I believe the real problem comes in, is that it almost always involves sexual fantasies of some sort—and a man who masturbates while thinking about a woman who is not his wife is engaging in what might be referred to as "mental infidelity."

Throughout the history of the church, different theologies have arisen concerning the relationship between the spiritual and the physical. "All things being created good to be enjoyed" expresses one end of the spectrum, and "to deny one's flesh in matters of food, sex, and comfort" represents the other.

There are scriptures that can be used to support both extremes and every shade of belief in between. It truly is up to the believer to pray, discern the Holy Spirit in it, and seek God's guidance. Good men may still disagree.

Most importantly, God's grace must always be modeled when dealing with those suffering from the compulsions of the flesh, no matter what those compulsions might be. There is no stronger denial of Christ than the self-righteous attitude of the holier-than-thou.

Sexual compulsivity is best explained in the words of someone who has struggled to overcome that compulsion.

"Many of us felt inadequate, unworthy, alone, and afraid. Our outsides never matched what we saw on the outside of others. Early on we came to feel disconnected—from parents, from peers, from ourselves. We tuned out with fantasy and masturbation. We plugged in by drinking in the pictures, the images, and pursuing the objects of our fantasies. We lusted and wanted to be lusted after.

"We became true addicts: sex with self, promiscuity, adultery, dependency relationships, and more fantasy. We got it through the eyes: We bought it, we sold it, we traded it, we gave it away. We were addicted to the intrigue, the tease, the forbidden. The only way we knew to be free of it was to do it. 'Please connect with me and make me whole!' we cried with outstretched arms. Lusting after the Big Fix, we gave away our power to others.

"This produced guilt, self-hatred, remorse, emptiness, and pain, and we were driven ever inward, away from reality, away from love, lost inside ourselves.

"Our habit has made true intimacy impossible. We could never know real union with another because we were addicted to the unreal." [6]

Although you may have to begrudgingly admit that you may be sexually compulsive at times, you still might be reluctant to read the next chapter—which discusses alcohol. But please do.

You may not be a drinker yourself, but part of understanding compulsivity entails understanding the problem drinker. In fact, many men who struggle with compulsivity had an alcoholic parent.

Perhaps you know a man in your family who drinks too much. Maybe it's your father, or perhaps a brother. Read on and see how his drinking affects you!

I mention

6

WHAT'S SO BAD ABOUT A LITTLE DRINK?

So far, we have talked about two of the three compulsions that defeat most men: work and sex.

In this chapter I am going to talk about the third area that seems to especially invite compulsive behavior. Then, in the following chapters, we'll go on to talk in more detail about specific ways to overcome compulsive behavior in these areas.

The third area is alcohol.

Your first reaction when I mention alcohol may tend to be, "That shouldn't be a problem for a Christian."

If that's how you feel, let me tell you about Robert.

Robert was a successful business executive—a man who was dedicated to God, and his church . . . who would never think of doing anything sinful or immoral.

And yet, because of his position in the business world, Robert often found himself at social functions where the wine and mixed drinks were flowing—where there wasn't *anyone* who didn't have a glass in his or her hand.

At first, he contented himself with orange juice. But he really felt a little out of place, and a little conspicuous.

He didn't really see anything wrong with having a glass of wine now and then. After all, he knew that Jesus had turned water into wine . . . and that the apostle Paul had told Timothy to drink a little wine for his stomach's sake . . . so he didn't see how anyone could say that an occasional drink was a "sin."

And so it was that he exchanged his orange juice for something with a little more "bite" to it.

It didn't take long for Robert to discover that he liked the feeling he got when he drank. He felt mellow, and relaxed, and better able to cope with the pressures of his career.

Before long, Robert's drinking wasn't confined to social functions. The first thing he did when he got home at the end of a hard day was to pour himself a drink. Sometimes two drinks. Or even three.

Robert never really drank to excess. But just the same, his drinking was becoming a compulsion. He was beginning to feel that he *needed* alcohol to help him *unwind*, after a hard day. Well, the truth was that he needed it to help him unwind after an easy day, too.

But if he hadn't received the help he needed, who knows where he might have wound up. Perhaps like Joe.

MARSHA AND JOE

Sometimes, having an alcoholic in your life can be just as bad as being one yourself—especially if you're married to one.

When Marsha first came to see me, I thought she had a problem with drinking. Although she was well-dressed, her hair was dishevelled, her eyes were red, and she generally looked like a wreck.

But it wasn't Marsha who had the problem. It was Joe, her husband.

Marsha explained that her husband had once been a dedicated Christian. He had been the type of man who was in church every time the doors were opened, and he had done everything he could to talk to their neighbors about the Lord.

But then some things happened that turned Joe's attitude upside down. There had been a split in the church over some issue that seemed to Joe to be totally insignificant. When the split occurred, it was not an amicable one. It was Christian against Christian, with angry passion spewing everywhere.

At first Joe was sad. Then he was appalled. And, finally, he was plain furious. He swore that he would never set foot inside another church. It is common for alcoholics to blame anything but themselves for their drinking. While going through a painful church split can be disillusioning, it wouldn't be likely that it could produce alcoholism. Yet, someone who is at risk for alcoholism will blame anything they can.

The more he drank, the more bitter he became. He was angry and abusive toward his wife and his children . . . as if he somehow blamed them for the disillusionment he had suffered.

Marsha had told Joe that she was going to take the children and move out of the house unless he came in for marriage counseling. He had agreed, with one stipulation. The counselor had to be a man. He wasn't about to waste his time with a "female shrink." That's why Marsha had come to me.

Even though she made her husband an appointment for a couple of days later, I really didn't think he would keep it. I was surprised when he did. But when he came into my office, it was immediately obvious that he did not want to be there.

He sat down, crossing his legs and folding his arms in front of him in a defensive and hostile posture.

"So, what brings you to counseling?" I asked.

"My wife thinks I've got a problem," he shrugged.

"So you're having trouble in your marriage?"

"*I'm* not having trouble with anything." He fairly spat the words at me. "I don't have a problem. Look, I know Marsha told you that I'm an alcoholic . . . but she's crazy. Sure, I drink a little bit, but who doesn't? And if she didn't nag me all the time, I probably wouldn't drink as much as I do."

When I asked him to tell me, in his opinion, what made a person an alcoholic, he said, "Well, that's a person who can't control it—gotta have it every day, you know, like a drug addict or a junkie. I didn't drink for two whole months once, so I *can't* be an alcoholic."

He went on to tell me that he had a brother who was an alcoholic and had gone to a rehabilitation center.

"That was fine for him. He had a problem with booze, and now he doesn't drink anymore. Me? I've never had a problem to begin with."

As to the extent of his drinking, he was proud that, "I don't even have a drop until in the evening. Then I just have a six-pack and a few shots of whiskey. Maybe a little more on the weekends."

Before I could say that it sounded like quite a bit of drinking to me, he quickly added, "But I can handle it. It's *never* been a problem!"

Following the Bible's advice to "speak the truth in love," I decided to tell him what I was thinking.

"Well, Joe, you know, from what you've told me you've been drinking every night for quite a while."

"So?"

"You know, there's a saying that if it quacks like a duck, walks like a duck, looks like a duck, and flies like a duck . . . then maybe it *is* a duck."

"What do you mean?" he demanded angrily.

"I'm saying that maybe you *are* an alcoholic. Maybe your wife is right. Have you ever considered that possibility?"

He stood up and pointed his finger in my face. "No! I told you, the only problem in my life is my wife . . . and *her* crazy ideas."

He turned and stormed out of my office. I never saw him, or Marsha, again.

I would like to think that he has at least taken the time to think the situation over more carefully. Otherwise, he is going to wind up a very lonely and sick man—estranged from his wife, and alienated from his children. Alcoholism can be a very lonely disease.

And what makes Joe's situation even sadder is that deep down inside he feels as if he's a victim. His drinking was brought about by "Christians" who couldn't live up to the name, but who let him down by their angry, vindictive, and un-Christlike behavior.

But the reality is that Joe is not a victim at all.

No one is responsible for Joe's drinking but Joe himself. What he must do is stop blaming others, take responsibility for his own actions, and find the resources to help him overcome the hurtful behavior.

What about you? Do you ever see yourself as a victim. It very well may be that you have good reason to feel angry, or hurt, or sad.

But none of that means you have to be a victim. You can take responsibility for your own pain and loss, deal with it in a proper way, and be spiritually whole and mature *in spite* of it.

What Is Alcoholism?

Alcoholism is probably one of the most widely misunderstood conditions in our society. Misinformation, myths, and stereotypes about what an alcoholic looks like and acts like have contributed to the confusion. There are many theories about what alcoholism is, but there is only one theory that has proven successful with regard to helping alcoholics stop drinking.

That theory is that alcoholism is a disease.

Really, it's more than a theory. It's the accepted definition, and it's what the American Medical Association declared in 1956. This "disease model" of alcoholism is the reason that Blue Cross and Blue Shield will pay for treatment of alcohol addiction.

Your desktop medical dictionary defines disease as "a morbid process with characteristic identifying symptoms regardless of whether the cause or likely outcome is known or unknown." Every student in medical school is taught to diagnose the symptoms of alcoholism. By definition, alcoholism is "a chronic disease, which is characterized by repeated use of alcoholic beverages to the extent that it exceeds normal dietary use, ordinary social customs, and which interferes with the interpersonal relationships or health of the drinker. Alcoholism is defined by the compulsive use of the chemical, loss of control, and continued use despite adverse consequences."

As a disease, alcoholism has three specific characteristics:

1. It is chronic.
2. It is progressive.
3. It is deadly.

Let me explain: First, *it is chronic.* Alcoholism is an un-usual disease in that it isn't caused by a germ or virus. But, like Type 1 diabetes, it usually appears early in a person's life and lasts throughout it. In a sense, it is a disease that has to be managed and not cured. Although many Chris-tians claim that they have been immediately delivered from alcoholism by a sovereign act of God, this would certainly have to be the very rare exception to the rule. Statistically, clinicians know that three out of four people who try to stop drinking will be back to it within a nine-month to one-year period. This is a relapse rate of 75 percent, and it shows how strong a hold this disease can have over people.

The second thing about alcoholism is that *it is a pro-gressive disease.* Left untreated, it is going to get worse. I would imagine that most of us have heard a sad story or two from the lips of someone trying to overcome a drinking problem. Some people may achieve sobriety for months at a time, but then when they go back to drinking, their bodies react worse to the alcohol than they did before. Each bout of drinking seems to become more painful than the pre-vious one.

And, finally, *alcoholism is a deadly disease.* It can kill slowly, through deterioration of the liver, and it can kill quickly, through stroke or automobile accident. Half of all fatal traffic accidents occur because at least one of the drivers involved had impaired judgment due to his consumption of alcohol. One alcoholic I knew died when he staggered out into the cold night air of northern Minnesota in Feb-ruary. His family didn't find him until the next morning, frozen to death in the backyard.

A compulsion toward alcohol can kill more than just the body, too. It can kill marriages, families, careers, rela-tionships of all types—and, unless it is faced up to and dealt with, it can kill the spirit.

One of the symptoms of problem drinking is that an

alcoholic can sometimes put away amazing amounts of liquor. This macho ability in men is highly regarded in some parts of society, but it is nothing at all to be proud of. In fact, it is a danger sign. As Michael Elkin writes in his book *Families Under the Influence*, "All central nervous system depressants share the property of fostering a physiological tolerance in users, so that it takes increasing amounts of the drug to produce a given effect. Therefore, a person using alcohol regularly will tend to increase dosage over time."[1]

I can remember how, in high school and college, the mark of a "real man" was to be able to chug-a-lug prodigious amounts of beer, chased down with tequila or whiskey. The goal was to drink as much as possible without acting intoxicated or getting sick. This was easier, of course, for the alcoholics or pre-alcoholics among the group. Novices or social drinkers usually wound up getting violently ill and swearing off alcohol forever, or at least until the next weekend beer party.

From time to time I see a news report about some young man who has died, simply because he tried to win one of these drinking contests. Young adults don't understand how dangerous alcohol can be; and consumed in great quantities by someone who hasn't built up his resistance to the effects of it, it can be immediately lethal. But then, it is also lethal to the person who *has* built up an increased tolerance. It's just that it takes longer for the alcohol to kill him.

I often counsel young people who are becoming heavy drinkers, "When you stop throwing up after your beer parties and can handle your liquor better, you are most likely on your way toward alcoholic drinking."

An entire book could be written about all of the damage that alcohol does to the body. Some of the effects of drinking to excess include neuropathy, kidney problems, bloating, pancreatitis, enlarged liver, brain deterioration, osteoporosis, hypertension, alcoholic hepatitis, and even cancer of the esophagus.[2] Alcohol, although it may be disguised in a sweet-tasting beverage, is a colorless and odorless poison. It usually doesn't kill you as quickly as would arsenic or cyanide—but it does the job just the same.

The Problem of Denial

"Denial is the first line of defense for any compulsive behavior" writes author Thomas Whiteman, Ph.D. Before a man can begin to move into wholeness, he must first admit he has a problem. This seemingly simple truth can be sabotaged by the phenomenon of denial. Denial may take many forms, which I will describe later, but it is basically the refusal to accept the truth about one's true condition. Many pastoral counselors have observed that the greater the compulsion, the greater the denial. Until the denial begins to crumble, progress is impossible.

Denial, as an automatic defense mechanism, was built into the soul by God to protect us from trauma that might overwhelm our ability to survive. For instance, suppose Charles and Hank are charging across a battlefield during wartime. As Charles watches in horror, his companion Hank takes a direct hit from a mortar round. Charles's life is also in danger and he automatically goes into denial so he can keep running for cover. There is no time to grieve, only time to survive, and denial can help him accomplish this.

Denial can protect us from overload. Yet, for the compulsive who has yet to admit his powerlessness, it is as if his denial button is stuck in the "on" position. Denial tells him that there is no problem, he's in control, "no sweat." The walls of denial keep out the Holy Spirit, others, and even keeps us cut off from our own true self.

Denial can take many forms, but especially manifests itself in the following five ways:

1. comparing with others
2. rationalizing
3. short-term control
4. listening to enablers
5. blaming others

Comparing with others. Marsha's husband Joe did this

when he told me about his brother, who had gone to an alcohol treatment center to get help. "Now my brother . . . *he* was an alcoholic. But I'm not."

The compulsive drinker is forever trying to take attention away from his own behavior and focus it on someone else.

"Why, my uncle Joe . . . he used to down a fifth of vodka every day—and he had to have it. I'm not like that. I just enjoy my liquor."

He points a finger at the wino on the street and says, "Look at that guy! Now that's an alcoholic. I have a job . . . I pay my bills . . . Now, how in the world can you accuse *me* of being an alcoholic?"

It is true that some compulsive drinkers seem to have more trouble in life than others. They appear to be "sicker." Truthfully, though, it's just that they have become less and less adept at hiding their disease, *and* the alcohol has taken more and more control over their actions. And remember, alcoholism is a progressive disease.

I'm not sure which is sadder—the drunk on the street, or the drunk with a home, wife, and family who refuses to see his behavior for what it really is. Ultimately, they are both headed toward destruction.

Nobody else's behavior has the power to determine what *you* do.

Your Uncle Joe's an alcoholic? What does that have to do with your own behavior? You used to know a guy who drank a pint of whiskey every day? What does that have to do with you drinking a half pint every day? The answer to both of these questions is the same: *absolutely nothing.*

The problem drinker must be made to see that he is responsible for his own behavior, regardless of what anyone else does.

Rationalizing. Another way compulsive drinkers excuse their behavior is by finding a reason for it.

I've heard excuses like, "Well, I'm under a lot of stress on the job right now, and that's why I'm drinking so much. As soon as things calm down, I'll stop." Or, "I really don't drink that much, except during the holidays. Once we get past Christmas (or Independence Day, or Thanksgiving, or Labor Day, or any other holiday you can think of) I'll be fine."

A person like this always has a reason for his drinking—and he can find an excuse any time he needs one!

Just up ahead he sees the "light at the end of the tunnel," and plans to stop drinking when he gets there, but he never seems to get there. He needs to realize that there is really *no excuse* for drinking, and there is only one time to stop drinking, and that is right now!

Besides, the person who says that he is only drinking because of some temporary difficulty or painful situation is showing that he is truly compulsive. He is "medicating his pain" with alcohol, just as the compulsive worker does by overdoing it on the job, and the person who is sexually compulsive does by engaging in promiscuity.

Short-term control. The third of the five ways through which the compulsive drinker is able to convince himself that he doesn't really have a problem is by abstaining for a short while.

He may go without drinking for a few days or a week, just to prove to himself that he can do it, but then he goes right back to it.

What I hear from this person is usually something like, "I can quit drinking anytime I want to. I just don't want to." But he will point to those few days without alcohol as proof that he is not addicted.

This is one of the excuses used by Marsha's husband, Joe. He felt that he couldn't possibly be an alcoholic because he had been able to go for a week or two without a drink at one time in his life. Not only that, but he was proud of the fact that he *never* had a drink before evening. After all, if he was able to go through the workday without a drink, wasn't that proof positive that he was not an alcoholic? Surely an alcoholic couldn't exercise that much control. He had an erroneous perception of what an alcoholic is and how such a person behaves.

Short-term abstinence through sheer willpower can actually be dangerous, because it convinces the alcoholic that hc has control over his drinking—rather than the other way around. It is precisely when he thinks he's strongest that he's likely to be sucked under.

It is only when he accepts his powerlessness over his addiction and admits that there is a real problem that he can experience lasting sobriety.

Many alcoholics can summon up enough willpower to abstain for a while, but not for the long haul. A good question to ask yourself is whether or not you could abstain for the rest of your life. If the thought of never taking another drink causes you anxiety—and perhaps a little sweat on your upper lip—then you can be pretty sure that you are a compulsive drinker.

What an alcoholic usually doesn't realize is that his compulsive, self-defeating personality type is not cured just because he is not indulging in his addiction. Even if he is currently sober, he may still be manipulative, angry, and defensive—thus exhibiting all of the character traits of the person who *is* drinking. In counseling circles, the person who behaves this way is considered to be a "dry drunk." He has not dealt with the bigger issue, which involves the reason or reasons he started drinking in the first place— and until he does that, he will not improve his true condition. (Notice that I said he needs to deal with the *reason*— and that means digging deeper than the surface *excuses* he uses to justify his drinking.)

Remember the erroneous approaches to thinking and behavior we talked about in chapter 1? The alcoholic who thinks that he can just snap his fingers one day, stop drinking, and thus quit being an alcoholic, has fallen victim either to the "Just-Do-It" Approach, which says, "all it takes is willpower," or the "Tough-Guy" Approach, which says, "the macho man has to do it himself!" It's not that simple, and it doesn't work that way. Recovery is a process, and not a single event.

For counselors, a sure warning sign is an addict who gets better too quickly. In reality, he may not have gotten better at all. He may just be in remission, so to speak. When the compulsive person gets overconfident and feels that he no longer has a problem with whatever once had him bound, then he is a likely candidate for a relapse.

The apostle Paul spoke wisely when he said, "Beware when you think you stand, lest you fall."[3]

Listening to enablers. If the road to hell is paved with good intentions, that is doubly true of the road to alcoholism. What I mean by that is that the compulsive drinker is often assisted in his denial, and thus enabled to continue with his drinking, by well-meaning family members and friends.

For example, the alcoholic's wife may think she's doing her husband a favor by calling and telling the boss that he has the flu, when the truth is that he's just too hung-over to go to work. Her intention is to keep her husband out of trouble, but he would be better off if she'd tell the truth and let him face the consequences.

The friends of a compulsive drinker may think that if they use positive-thinking, praise, and encouragement, their friend will be helped, but always the opposite is true. What the alcoholic needs is to be confronted by the truth, and to be held responsible for his own actions, not to be treated with kid gloves and have his behavior excused.

As long as he has people who are going to be there to pick up after him, make excuses for him, and bail him out of any trouble he might drink himself into, he's never going to change. Why should he?

I realize that it is hard *not* to be an enabler for two reasons: first of all, because it is hard to see someone you love get himself into trouble. When your husband or son, or perhaps even your father, calls you from jail, tells you he's been picked up for drunk driving and asks you to come bail him out, it's difficult to say, "No . . . I can't do that right now." It seems rather like a betrayal to tell the boss, "Joe isn't coming to work today because he's got a terrible hangover," but if it will force the habitual drinker to face up to the results of his drinking, then that is what must be done.

The second reason it may be difficult to stop enabling the alcoholic or compulsive drinker is that it is embarrassing for the wife, child, or parent of the alcoholic to admit to the problem. It can be almost as hard for the spouse of the alcoholic to admit her husband's drinking problem as it is for the husband to admit it.

She doesn't want her friends to feel sorry for her, or to look down on her. And she's afraid they might if they knew. So she tends to put on a happy face and pretend that "everything is fine, thank you."

The wife may also be in denial, because to admit that her husband is an alcoholic is to admit that things are not going to get better until and unless he gets help—and she doesn't want to believe that. She wants to think that his drinking is only a temporary thing brought on by current circumstances. That way, she can tell herself that as soon as those circumstances pass, his drinking will stop, along with whatever difficult behavior it causes: verbal abuse, physical violence, disinterest in sex, depression, etc.

Remember, if you know someone who you think might be an alcoholic, you're not doing him any favor by covering up for him.

I must point out here that the alcoholic's behavior can be just as destructive to his wife and children as it is to himself.

Often, the wife of an alcoholic will develop "counter-symptoms" such as migraine headaches, obesity, depression, or she will become involved in an obsessive-compulsive behavior of her own. Michael Elkin writes, "The fact that such a woman necessarily has very strong feelings that must be repressed and suppressed can account for her symptoms psychodynamically."

He adds that the wife of an alcoholic generally "has low self-esteem with a very dependent personality framework. . . . It is not likely that a person with high self-esteem would put up with a fraction of what an alcoholic's wife routinely tolerates."[4]

In listing a "job description" for the wife of the alcoholic, Elkins says that, among other things, she must have the "capacity to never ask, 'What's in this for me?' The ability to do enormous amounts of work for a minimal payoff. Resilience with a high tolerance to pain. Stability, and resistance to panic."[5]

From this description you can see why it is very easy
for the wife of the alcoholic to move into a state of denial
herself, because the reality she lives with is often so brutal.
The children may also become very adept at avoiding reality. They may become compulsive in other ways: For instance, they may become compulsively neat, compulsively
controlling in their relationships with others (since they
can't control at all what their father does), or, they may
model their father's behavior, and wind up as alcoholics
themselves.

Living with an alcoholic who is in denial can be an awful
experience—a life filled with sorrow, insecurity, anxiety,
shame, and perhaps violence. Anyone who is in this position should seek out counseling help for herself and her
children, even if the compulsive drinker himself refuses to
get help.

Blaming others. Once again, I refer you back to Joe, who
blamed his wife Marsha: "If she didn't nag me all the time,
I probably wouldn't drink as much as I do," he had told
me.

I could fill a book with the excuses I've heard from
compulsive drinkers who absolutely refused to take responsibility for their own actions. Here are a few:

- "My boss is such a jerk! He puts so much pressure on
  me, I just *have* to have a couple of drinks at the end
  of the day to unwind."
- "My kids make so much noise, running in and out of
  the house—slamming doors—playing their music so
  loud . . . why it's enough to drive *anyone* to drink!"
- "I wouldn't drink at all if my wife would at least *try*
  to see my point of view once in a while."

There may be a glimmer of truth in some of these excuses. That's precisely what makes them so dangerous. The
little bit of truth is what enables the compulsive drinker to
believe the rest of the lie!

Remember, please, that no one is responsible for your
behavior but you. Unless someone is putting a gun to your
head and forcing you to take a drink, then it's just not fair

to blame anyone else for what you're doing. All of the things you're saying may be true. Your boss may be a jerk! Your wife may be a nag. Your kids may make so much noise that it gives you a whopper of a headache. But not one of those things—or even all of them taken together— is a valid excuse for taking refuge in a bottle of booze.

Are You a Compulsive Drinker?

Keeping in mind what I've been saying about denial, answer the following questions to see if you might have a problem with compulsive drinking. Or, if you're worried about someone you know or love, see how you think they would answer these questions, if they were to answer them honestly.

_____ Do you ever drink alone?

_____ Have you ever stopped using one drug—such as marijuana or cocaine—only to substitute another (such as alcohol)?

_____ Do you drink regularly (every night, several times per week, or every weekend)?

_____ Do you find yourself avoiding people or places that don't approve of your drinking?

_____ Have there ever been any financial or legal consequences from your drinking?

_____ Have you ever tried to stop drinking—or to at least ease up on it?

_____ Does the thought of never having another drink again for the rest of your life cause you feelings of anxiety?

_____ Has anyone ever suggested to you that you might have a drinking problem?

_____ Have you ever felt guilty, defensive, or ashamed of your drinking?

_____ Do you ever use alcohol to alleviate stress or to help you relax?

_____ Do you regularly drink more than sixteen ounces of beer or wine at one sitting?

If you answered yes to two or more of these questions, then you have a problem with compulsive drinking.

Getting Rid of Denial

What if you see yourself in this chapter—if you realize that you *do* have a problem with compulsive behavior when it comes to alcohol? What can you do about it?

Seek counseling from a certified addictions counselor, or from a counselor who specializes in compulsivity problems and is learned in addiction treatment. It would be preferable if the counselor has overcome some addictions or is at least involved personally in a growth process. And equally important, it would be helpful if the counselor could pray with you.

I recommend, first of all, that you get involved in a Twelve-Step Program, such as one run by Alcoholics Anonymous. We will be talking more about the Twelve Steps when we get to chapter 8, so I won't spend any time talking about them now, except to say that over the years they have been effective in liberating thousands of men and women from bondage to alcoholism and other compulsive behaviors. Although Alcoholics Anonymous is not overtly Christian in its outlook—referring to a "higher power" instead of to Christ—the Twelve Steps can still be used effectively by and for Christians. In fact, some churches and other Christian organizations have had success with a modified version of the Twelve Steps that *does* acknowledge Christ as the higher power upon which freedom from bondage ultimately depends.

You can probably find a good Twelve-Step Program in your area by looking up Alcoholics Anonymous in the white pages of your telephone book. There may also be an alcohol hotline, or you can look in the yellow pages under Alcohol Abuse.

The alcoholic who is involved in a Twelve-Step Program and/or one-on-one counseling, who is serious about it and perseveres, may soon begin to see marked improvement in his attitude and behavior. His denial will begin to crumble so that he can face up to and deal with the truth.

Remember, though, that three out of four alcoholics or drug addicts go back to their addiction within a year of stopping. So stick with the program. The first year of sobriety can be extremely difficult as the family learns to live together again. In their book *Love Is a Choice,* Drs. Robert Hemfelt, Frank Minirth, and Paul Meier write, "In counsel we warn couples carefully that the first year into sobriety is a killer. Three to nine months after Dad dries out, the family will find themselves beset by crises. . . .

"But if the family hangs together, staying in recovery together to weather that first stormy year, the healing will seem miraculous. Wonderful!"[6]

But even after that first stormy year, don't think you've got it made and that you'll never become a compulsive drinker again. If you are an alcoholic now, you will always need to think of yourself as someone who can't afford to take that first drink—because you can't be certain where it's going to lead. Even if you have dealt completely with the underlying pain in your life, and feel that you could no longer be bound in the least by compulsive behavior, it is still much better to be safe than sorry.

If you are a Christian, I urge you to take seriously Paul's command, "Do not get drunk on wine, which leads to debauchery. Instead be filled with the Spirit."[7]

Now that we have discussed the three compulsions that defeat most men, we're going to move on to a discussion of some of the inner emotional states that drive men to seek refuge in compulsive behavior. We're going to talk about things like grief, rage, and shame.

7
THE REAL NEED

Looking across the table into Ellen's sparkling eyes, Bruce felt a flood of happiness and contentment.

He knew this evening was long overdue. He had been working much too hard lately, and he realized that. But now he was giving his wife the evening out she deserved— the evening she had waited for so long.

This restaurant was going to set him back plenty. It was one of the most expensive places in town . . . but judging by the happy, loving look on Ellen's face, it was going to be more than worth every penny.

And then . . . just like always . . . everything began to unravel.

It all began because Bruce didn't get what he had ordered.

Glaring down at his plate, he summoned the waiter. "This is *not* what I ordered," Bruce said, in a tone that was just a little nastier than it needed to be.

"I'm sorry, sir," the waiter began, "but I thought—"

Bruce interrupted him. "I told you—this is *not* what I ordered. And you'd better do something about it or I'm not paying for this dinner."

"Yes, sir . . . I'm sorry."

The waiter's apology didn't seem to make a difference in Bruce's attitude.

Suddenly, he turned his attention to his wife's steak.

"And look at this! She asked for medium well! You call *this* medium well?"

Ellen looked at the floor. "Really . . . it's okay, honey."

"No, it's not okay! You come to a place like this, you should at least get what you order."

By now the waiter had hurried back into the kitchen to "fix" both their dinners, but Bruce was still fuming.

When he continued to grumble about things, Ellen said, in a pleading voice, "Bruce . . . please . . . you're embarrassing me."

That did it.

"I'm embarrassing you? Great! I take you out to the best restaurant in town, and now you're ashamed of me."

"I didn't say I was ashamed—" she pleaded, but she let her sentence drop. She knew that it didn't take a whole lot to set Bruce off, and when it happened, all you could do was stay out of his way.

When their dinners came back from the kitchen, they ate without saying two words to each other—and the ride home was no pleasure drive. Bruce drove fast, and stopped a little too suddenly when a light turned red, just to let his "ungrateful" wife know how angry he was.

As soon as he screeched the car to a stop in their driveway, Ellen was out the door, into the house, and into the bedroom, slamming the door behind her.

Bruce was still angry as he followed her into the house—but then he heard her crying, and it hit him, just as it always did.

I can't believe I did it again, he thought to himself as he sunk down onto the living room sofa. *What in the world is wrong with me? I wanted to show her a good time. And now she thinks I'm a real jerk.*

He sighed. "And I guess she's right."

Is Anybody in There?

Tim was a direct contrast to Bruce. Whereas Bruce seemed to fly off the handle at the slightest provocation, Tim never got angry about anything—even when he had a good reason. Tim was quiet, introspective, and really didn't seem to have an opinion about anything. Those who knew him often remarked that he seemed to be "sad," like a lost little boy.

Just the other day, in a department store, Tim had picked up a coat he was thinking about buying. It was the last one on the rack, and it was just the type of coat he had been looking for.

But before he could try it on, a loud voice behind him said, "Hey, pal . . . I was going to buy that coat."

"What?" Tim turned to look into an angry, belligerent face.

"The coat. I was going to buy it. It's mine!"

"Oh," Tim said. "I'm sorry. Here." He meekly handed the coat over.

The other man took it without so much as "Thanks."

A salesperson, who had been watching the whole thing, came up and whispered in Tim's ear.

"Why did you let *him* have the coat. *You* had it first."

Tim shrugged. "I don't know," was all he could say.

The salesperson didn't know how badly Tim had wanted to stand up for himself. He just couldn't do it. And so this type of thing happened to him all the time.

More than once, one of his friends had remarked about Tim that "there didn't seem to be anyone in there." And he felt pretty much the same way they did about himself.

What Tim didn't realize was that he was bound by a profound sense of grief, sadness, and feelings of worthlessness. And until he begins to acknowledge those feelings, he will continue to set himself up to find relief through the self-destructive behavior that causes him such guilt.

Tim and Bruce had one thing in common. They were both out of touch with their feelings. And this led to major problems in their relationships with God, themselves, and others.

It's been said that it's easy to hurt others when you can't feel pain yourself. And that's basically what was going on with Bruce and Tim.

Men who are out of touch with their feelings appear to

be insensitive to others, and especially to women, because women *are* generally more aware of their emotions and feelings, and have a need to be understood and related to on that level. But many men have medicated their pain for so many years that they honestly don't have the slightest idea as to why they behave as they do.

It is interesting to me that when I ask a man in counseling how he feels about something, he will almost always tell me what he *thinks*.

The dialogue usually goes something like this:

"Tell me, how do you feel about your father's death?"

"Well, I *think* that death happens to everyone, eventually."

"Yes, but how do you *feel* about his dying?"

"I . . . uh, *think* that death is just a natural part of life, and it's just something that we all have to accept."

"Why is it that when I ask you how you feel, you tell me what you *think*? What I'm interested in finding out is how you really *feel* about it."

"Oh." There will be a brief silence, which is usually followed by, "I haven't really *thought* about it."

Yet men do have feelings. To be human is to have emotions, and since men are human, we know that the feelings are in there, somewhere. And even when those emotions are not being given expression, when they are buried far beneath the surface, they are still there. In fact, ignoring or suppressing emotions only increases their ability to affect us. In counseling circles there is a saying: "What you don't deal with deals with you." In other words, internalized pain is the fuel that fires the flames of compulsive behavior.

In order to overcome compulsive behavior, you must first identify the underlying need or pain that is causing the behavior. There are several basic and very common emotional states that men medicate to keep from feeling the pain.

These states include shame, grief, rage, fear, mistrust, and codependency. To understand a man's behavior, one must understand these powerful forces; and especially shame, grief, and anger.

The Problem of Shame

Much has been written over the past few years about the emotion of shame. Shame that has not been dealt with may be the single biggest catalyst for addictive and compulsive behavior.

Healthy shame contributes to the development of spirituality. But unhealthy shame puts a man in bondage to a standard that he can never live up to. Shame has been described as "a feeling deep within that makes us want to hide."[1]

The apostle Paul, who had so many insights into human behavior, put it like this: "Godly sorrow brings repentance that leads to salvation, and leaves no regret, but worldly sorrow brings death."[2] In other words, healthy shame will prompt a man to realize how dependent he is upon the grace of God, and will move him toward, instead of away from, the Lord. Unhealthy shame will prompt a man to feel that he is worthless, no good, and that he might as well give up. No matter how hard he might try, or what he might do to punish himself, he simply cannot assuage his guilt. Jane Middleton-Moz calls this "debilitating guilt."

"In normal guilt one feels relief from guilt when punished or when amends can be made. In debilitating guilt, however, punishment can never be attained, even through consistent self-punishment or self-deprivation."[3]

Unhealthy shame allows a man to continue his bad habits. He figures that he's "bad to the bone" anyway, and the guilt he feels just sets him up to experience the vicious cycle of addiction. His shame is compounded every time he engages in whatever compulsive activity it is that has him bound.

He may experience a temporary alleviation of shame, or a high during his compulsive behavior, but afterwards he feels such an intensity of self-loathing that it can almost destroy him.

Of all the human conditions that I have encountered as a therapist, I believe the number one dysfunction among Christian people is their failure to truly love themselves. In fact, many of the men with whom I have worked have actually hated themselves. Basically, they have not accepted the fact that they are human. Because of intense feelings of shame, they may see themselves as wimps or worms, or they may go to the other extreme, and attempt to make up for their perceived shortcomings by trying to act like Rambo or some other unreal symbol of manhood. They really don't have any idea of what manhood is all about—what it means to have dignity, self-respect, and healthy self-esteem. They may tend to tell lies about anything and everything—even the most trivial matters—because the truth is always perceived to be threatening to them.[4]

Looking at it from a biblical perspective, these are people who are focused on law, rather than grace. They perceive that God is disappointed in them, and so they cannot enter into His rest. They are constantly striving in one way or another, until they may just give up and drop out. It's not that they've lost their faith, but they don't see any reason to keep on fighting a perpetually losing battle. Because these men tend to see spirituality as something they "do," rather than something they "receive" from God, they can become hypercritical of themselves and of others.

They have few, if any, real friends because it is impossible to let another person get close to you if you have rejected yourself.

Shame often results from the way a person was treated by his parents when he was a child. If a child was often ridiculed, laughed at, looked down upon, and made to feel inferior, he is almost certainly going to grow into an adult who is bound by the emotion of shame. From psychologist Jane Middleton-Moz comes this list of characteristics of adults who were shamed in their childhoods:[5]

1. Adults shamed as children are afraid of vulnerability and fear exposure of self.
2. They may suffer extreme shyness, embarrassment,

and feelings of being inferior to others. They don't believe they *make* mistakes. Instead they believe they *are* mistakes.

3. They fear intimacy and tend to avoid real commitment in relationships.
4. They may appear to be either self-centered or selfless.
5. They feel that they will always be "worthless and unlovable."
6. They tend to feel defensive when even minor negative feedback is given.
7. They tend to blame others before anyone has a chance to blame them.
8. They feel guilty and apologize constantly.
9. They feel like outsiders and often have a pervasive sense of loneliness throughout their lives, even when surrounded by those who love and care for them.
10. They project their negative beliefs about themselves onto others, and are constantly feeling judged by others as a result.
11. They feel angry and judgmental toward the qualities in others that they feel ashamed of in themselves.
12. They often feel ugly, flawed, and imperfect.
13. They may be controlled and lack the ability to be spontaneous.
14. They may feel that they must do things perfectly or not at all, with the result that they feel performance anxiety and procrastinate.
15. They are often depressed.
16. They may lie to themselves and others.
17. They may block their feelings of shame through compulsive behaviors like workaholism, eating disorders, substance abuse, etc.
18. They tend to have "caseloads" rather than "friendships."

19. They may feel constantly violated by others.

Shame can be a terrible taskmaster.

The Problem of Grief

Another hidden emotion that tends to keep men from being what they want to be is grief. Many men are completely out of touch with their sadness.

When a little boy is hurt, or has his feelings hurt, he will usually be quick to tell you that he is mad or sad. But, unfortunately, by the time that same boy reaches puberty he has learned not to feel his anger or sadness. And even if he does feel it, he knows that he's not supposed to tell anyone about it.

He hears things like, "Big boys don't cry," or "Come on, son, that didn't hurt you! Be a man about it."

The implication is that *real* men don't feel pain or show their emotions. To admit to hurt or emotional pain is somehow seen as sissy behavior—acceptable for girls, but certainly not for boys.

Sometimes, a boy will try so hard to be a man that he reaches the point where he will refuse to admit that he feels anything at all.

Why do so many men have so much sadness inside of them? There are numerous things that can contribute to a man's sense of loss throughout his life. Still, it is most likely that the cause of grief in a man lies in his relationship with his own father. The grief of being abandoned, abused, shamed, or betrayed by a father who failed to nurture his son can be overwhelming.

A man's ability to be intimate with his male friends (if he has any), his wife, and his children, is often a direct reflection of how close he was to his own father. If his father was distant, critical, overbearing, violent, or absent, the son is probably going to be the same way with his own children. He doesn't want to be that way . . . but he just doesn't know how to behave differently.

I can't count the number of male clients I have worked

with who have told me that they never really knew their fathers. Dad may have been there physically during the growing-up years, but emotionally he was somewhere else. He was just not able to relate on an intimate, heart-to-heart basis. Invariably, these clients would tell themselves that they weren't going to be like their fathers when they grew up—but now here they were, acting in the very same way.

You see, a man provides a role model for his sons. If they don't learn intimacy from the man who means the most in their life, they may doubt that intimacy is important at all. They will also lack in the ability to be intimate with others. And a man who does not deal with the unfinished business of his past relationship with his father is especially likely to become just like "the old man."

I have looked into the eyes of many men and seen a sad little boy. Men in recovery often find themselves weeping for unexplainable reasons. Often, hymns heard in church will cause the tears to flow. Or perhaps a sad movie might touch a sensitive wound.

Men have much to cry about—but they've been holding it all inside, compounding their pain and giving it more power to hold them in self-defeating behaviors. Often, a man who is learning to overcome compulsive behavior will be bewildered and a bit embarrassed when he begins to shed tears. He probably hasn't cried for many years—and perhaps didn't even think he was *capable* of crying. I am quick to assure such a person that crying is nothing at all to be ashamed of. Instead, tears are a sure sign that healing is beginning to take place.

The Problem of Rage

Show me a man who isn't angry about anything, and I'll show you a corpse!

In other words, there are hundreds of things to be angry about in this world of ours, and a man who isn't angry about anything is either emotionally dead, or else he's just not paying attention.

Anger comes to us because this world is not always fair

or predictable, and there are no guarantees. A man works hard to get that promotion, only to find that it went to the big boss's son-in-law. He invests in what everybody tells him is a strong stock, only to have the bottom fall out of it. He is a loyal and dedicated employee with years of service who is laid off at the first sign of tough economic times. These sorts of things happen all the time in this fallen world of ours.

A man's anger may come because he sometimes must deal with a very inconsistent universe. He is expected to be strong, resourceful, brave, and always on top of things. Men are sometimes shamed for being human by other men, and also shamed for being male by women.

The characteristics of the masculine psyche are often misunderstood and sometimes threatening to a woman, so when a mother sees them in her boy, she often reacts in a way that makes him feel angry and ashamed.

For example, the masculine psyche has a need to fight. Boys delight in making "swords" out of sticks and whacking the daylights out of one another. A mother may shame her son by yelling at him, "Stop that this instant! Why do you have to be so violent? Now, get in here and help me with the dishes!"

The last thing the boy needs is to be shamed for exhibiting the naturally aggressive tendencies of the male. What he does need is to have the guidance of an older male—preferably his father, of course—who can help him channel his natural energy and aggressiveness so that it can be used in constructive ways.

In the same way, adult anger must be channeled into constructive energy. Anger is not necessarily bad. Jesus himself was obviously angry when He drove the money-changers out of the temple. Historically, anger has led to many beneficial changes in our world—most recently, for instance, the fall of communism and the leveling of the Berlin Wall. What *is* bad about anger is what it can do to you—and other people—if it is mishandled and misdirected.

And too often, that's what happens. Anger becomes a destructive force that destroys from within, *and* lashes out in all directions, damaging relationships and ruining lives.

All younger men need someone older to show them proper ways of venting legitimate anger. Sadly, too many young men have seen just the opposite. They have grown up in homes where their fathers didn't have the slightest idea how to handle their own anger—with fathers who may have lashed out verbally or physically—and as a result they are bruised verbally, emotionally, and physically.

Sometimes, they may transfer their feelings of anger toward their fathers onto God himself. Drs. Hemfelt, Minirth, and Meier talk about one such person in their book, *Love Is a Choice.* The client was so upset by her feelings of antipathy toward God that she thought she must be demon possessed.

"Rebecca's daddy was a rigid, perfectionistic dentist, a military man. Every two years the family moved, from base to base, state to state, country to country. Rebecca never completed two full years in the same school. Her role was to smile and agree that whatever Daddy wanted, that's what the family should do. Neither she nor her mother was allowed to express anger, frustration, or hurt at having to put down roots and rip them out again.

"Now, years later, a part of her—the part that showed—loved God the Father. Indeed, Rebecca is a beautiful and committed Christian. But she was also getting in touch with the hidden part. The unresolved anger and resentment. She had transferred that ugly side of her relationship with her dad to her relationship with God. Because it was so incomprehensible to her that she might be angry with God, she assumed there must be some outside force within her."[6]

Some people believe that the best way to deal with anger is to "stuff it down inside and keep a lid on it." Unfortunately, anger that is turned inward is often transformed into depression, or it may "emerge sideways" in passive-aggressive actions—for example, the man who may not "mean to," but who always breaks a couple of dishes or a cup when his wife asks him to help her with the dishes.[7]

The Problem of Being Overly Controlling

Another problem that keeps many men bound is a tendency to be overly controlling in their relationships with others—especially their spouse.

If this person could honestly articulate the way he feels, he would tell the person he is trying so hard to control something like this:

"My good feelings about who I am stem from being liked by you and receiving your approval. Your clothing, behavior, and personal appearance, I believe, are a reflection on me—so you must allow me to control you. My energy is spent relieving your problems, soothing your pain, pleasing and protecting you, and, of course, manipulating you so that you do everything 'my way.'

"My self-esteem is strengthened by solving your problems, because you are a task that I take on to feel good about myself.

"I am not aware of how I feel; I wonder how you feel.

"I am not aware of what I want; I ask what you want.

"When I don't know what you want or feel, I assume.

"My fear of your anger and your possible rejection of me determines what I say or do. My social circle diminishes as I involve myself with you.

"There is something familiar to me about our relationship. It reminds me of how I took care of my mother/father growing up at the expense of my own development. I am a very controlling person. I don't understand when you don't want my help."[8]

This controlling compulsion has sometimes been called codependency, which may be defined as "the fallacy of trying to control interior feelings by controlling people, things, and events on the outside. To the codependent, control or the lack of it is central to every aspect of life."[9]

The controlling person can be very difficult to deal with because he won't tell you what his needs are. He just naturally expects you to know what they are, and will resent you if you do not meet them. It is hard for him to share his needs with a loved one because he is hypersensitive about the possibility of being rejected.

Codependent people have been described as being like "vacuum cleaners gone wild, drawing to themselves not just another person, but also chemicals (alcohol or drugs primarily) or things—money, food, sexuality, work. The struggle is relentless to fill the great emotional vacuum within themselves."[10]

It has been said that if you can't say no, then your yes doesn't really mean anything. The controlling person really can't say no to the object of his compulsion, whether that person is his parent, spouse, or girlfriend. The desire or need to stay attached doesn't stem from a mutually healthy interaction, but rather from a one-sided compulsion to feel needed.

Although a codependent relationship might look loving to the outsider, upon closer inspection, it can be seen that the relationship is really based on immaturity and emotional sickness. It certainly isn't based on love.

What sets the stage for someone to develop a compulsion to control? Usually, it starts in childhood when—due to sickness, alcoholism, or marital unhappiness—the child is forced to "take care" of Mommy or Daddy. In effect, the child becomes the "parent" and the parent becomes the "child." This compulsion can also develop when the child is forced to perform duties that the sick parent has abdicated, such as raising the younger children. This is damaging to the development of the older child who, upon reaching adulthood, unconsciously seeks out another person to take care of. He is not attracted to emotionally healthy and mature people, but finds himself instead in relationships where there is some need to "rescue" the other person.

In counseling, I have talked to many compulsively controlling men who married women who were emotionally weak or ill in some way. They entered into the marriage thinking that they could control and change the other person, but then were bitterly unhappy when they found out they couldn't.

I am not belittling their problems, because I have heard some woeful tales. But my reaction is, "Well, you picked her. Why did you marry such a wounded person? What was so familiar about her that made you feel comfortable with her? Could it be that your relationship with her is very similar to previous primary relationships in your life—say, with your mother or father?" Invariably, this proves to be true.

This compulsive need to control may also develop in a child who grows up in an environment where he is constantly being shamed, and who thus becomes "hypersensitive to the needs and demands of others in an attempt to remain invisible."[11]

In Christian circles there is quite a bit of confusion about codependency, and it's easy to see why. After all, Christians are called to be loving and giving—to care for their weaker brothers and sisters. This is what Jesus himself taught.

But there is a difference between the person who is truly loving and giving and the person who is "loving and giving" because he has a need to control the person who is on the receiving end of his "love" and "generosity." Real love is a choice one makes; codependency is a compulsion that comes from an inability to say no.

Codependency is like other compulsions in that it is an addiction to a person, or to the need to be liked and accepted by many persons. And the one who is truly compulsive in this area of his life will eventually become depressed, alcoholic, or physically sick, unless he becomes aware that he is caught in unhealthy relational patterns.

He is also likely to have a shallow relationship with God. When you get to know him, you will see that there is no spiritual serenity in his life, no "peace which transcends all understanding."[12]

From *Love Is a Choice:* "Two things may happen in a codependent's relationship with God. First, because of that polarizing filter, the person sees and hears only a narrow portion of God, not enough to get the necessary scope of both His judgment and His mercy. Moreover, the person cannot adequately perceive what *agape* (unconditional love) should be. Second, the person unconsciously tries to develop a relationship with Him on that limited or skewed basis.

"We most frequently see cases wherein the persons try to win God's approval with certain behaviors or rigid, self-imposed thought patterns. Anorexia is one such behavior. A rigid, stilted view of correct living is another. Sadly, because those persons never won the earthly parents' complete nurturance and approval, they never feel completely accepted by the Father. The best is never quite good enough. Frustration supplants godly love and contentment."[13]

Because we live in a fallen world, and most families are dysfunctional to one degree or another, just about everyone has some elements of the codependent personality. Many families have for years harbored things like alcoholism, physical sickness, marital stress, financial deprivation, perfectionism, unforgiveness, and sin. In fact, none of the conditions explained in this book should shock or embarrass you if you think you recognize yourself in them. To be human is to have unresolved issues, emotional wounds, or dysfunctional patterns of behavior. The real sickness lies, not in facing up to these problems, but in denying their existence.

The following questions are designed to help you see if there is underlying emotional pain of some type that is affecting your behavior—preventing you from relating to the world as you would like to. Don't be alarmed or surprised if you see that you have all of these emotional states in your life to one degree or another. Our aim here is to find out which one(s) is (are) dominant in your personality, and thus affecting your life to the greatest degree.

ANGER

1. Do you easily become upset in traffic?
2. Do you seethe about it if another driver "cuts you off"?
3. When you are angry with someone do you tend to ignore him?

4. Do you refuse to let people touch you?
5. Has anyone ever told you that you are critical?
6. Do you often go "looking for a fight"?
7. Do you anticipate the best from other people—or the worst?
8. Does it seem to you that other people have a much easier time of it than you do?
9. Do you have a hard time being patient?

Answering these questions *honestly* will give you a beneficial insight into your character. If you have more than two or three yes answers here, then you definitely have quite a bit of anger deep down inside of you. Four, five, or more yes answers indicate that you are extremely angry—whether or not you may realize it—and that you definitely need to face up to your anger. Question 3 is especially telling, because people who are harboring a great deal of anger tend to do just that . . . harbor it. They don't deal with it. The person who gets angry, but who quickly confronts the person who has offended him and gets it out in the open, is generally better able to deal with anger. The danger comes when anger is not dealt with, but pushed down deeper and deeper. Unless it is handled on a case-by-case basis, all that accumulated anger may explode some day—like a pressure cooker that has been left on the stove too long, or it will produce psychosomatically triggered illness.

SADNESS

1. Do you feel discouraged about your future?
2. Do you feel guilty about things—even when they may not be your fault?
3. Is it hard for you to make decisions?
4. Have others told you that you appear to be sad?
5. Do you have trouble sleeping?
6. Do you cry during movies?
7. Do you have trouble dealing with holidays like

Christmas and Thanksgiving? (Do you feel sad and lonely at holiday time?)

8. Do you often think wistfully about the old days when your life was better?
9. Do you sometimes feel depressed, like crying, but you don't know why?

Again, two or three yes answers indicates that you have some sadness inside of you. But remember what I said earlier . . . that most of us will have all of these traits to some degree. However, if you have four, five, or more yes answers to these questions, then sadness may be a real problem for you—something that's keeping you from getting everything out of life that life has to offer.

The sad person very often doesn't know *why* he feels sad. He just does. But only when he discovers the source of his grief and sadness, and faces up to it, can he overcome it, and live in freedom.

SHAME

1. Do you take yourself very seriously?
2. Are you critical of yourself and others?
3. Do you overdrink, overeat, or overindulge in sex?
4. Do you tend to be impulsive?
5. Do you start things, only to have trouble seeing them through to completion?
6. Do you find it difficult to play and have fun?
7. Do you have trouble loving and accepting yourself?
8. Are you afraid that others won't like you?
9. Have others ever told you that they wish you wouldn't put yourself down so much?

As with the questions regarding anger and sadness, two or three positive answers show there is some tendency on your part to feel shame about yourself. Four or five or more yes answers indicate that you need to discover the source of these negative feelings about yourself and deal with them once and for all. If you do have quite a few yes answers, let me assure you that you are not at all as bad as you think you are—and you can be set free from this terrible taskmaster.

NEED TO CONTROL

1. Are you overresponsible?
2. Are you afraid when other people feel anger toward you?
3. Do you have trouble expressing your wishes and desires in straightforward fashion?
4. Are you constantly afraid of being rejected?
5. Do you find yourself surrounded by people with problems?
6. Do you think you might be attracted to people with problems?
7. Has anyone ever accused you of being overly controlling?
8. Were you raised by a troubled parent?
9. Do you have trouble saying no?
10. Do you have a desperate need to be needed?

As I said earlier, this compulsion is sometimes hard to see, because on the surface this person may seem like a caring, compassionate Christian who delights in doing for other people. But it is all a matter of motive. This person doesn't really do for others—but for self. Only *you* can answer these questions honestly to see if you have a problem in this area. Please answer them as honestly as you possibly can, because freedom from a compulsive need to control others is essential for anyone who wants to have normal, happy, and healthy interpersonal relationships.

What did you find out from answering these questions? Is your predominant emotion anger, sadness, shame, or need to control?

The good news is that the minute we admit that we are experiencing one or more of these emotional states, we can step out of isolation and become authentic. We can then begin to connect with other men who have also struggled to break the bonds that hold them captive.

As this process continues, you will begin to find yourself being more honest with yourself, as well as with other people. In some cases, relationships may be temporarily strained as authentic emotions become part of your interactions with others.

A mature man is one who can acknowledge his true feelings, express himself appropriately, and then move on to the place of forgiveness and serenity.

In our next chapter we will examine a proven guide that will assist you in your walk toward greater inner health.

8
LOOKING TO GOD

If you are recovering from compulsive behavior of any kind, you are definitely not alone.

All across the world, millions of people are discovering that it is time to take deliberate and concrete steps to help themselves recover from personal, emotional, or relational difficulties.

Are you perfectionistic? Compulsive with regard to alcohol or other drugs? Is your sexual life out of control? Are you a compulsive worker? Someone who is overwhelmed by depression, rage, or sadness? Whatever your problem may be, there is hope! But those who gain solid ground are generally those who follow a well-defined program to help them overcome their compulsive behavior. It really is possible to overcome the problems that may have haunted you for years, but, as the old song says, "wishing and hoping" just won't do it. You've got to take specific action.

Whatever particular problems you may be dealing with, your journey toward wholeness needs to incorporate two specific items:

1. An awakening or intensifying of your spirituality, and your relationship with Jesus Christ.

2. Involvement in a Twelve-Step Program, preferably one that acknowledges the lordship of Christ over all human endeavor.

You may remember that we briefly discussed the Twelve-Step Program in chapter 4. These Twelve Steps have been used for years by groups like Alcoholics Anonymous, and they have been instrumental in bringing many people to victory over compulsive behavior. Utilizing a step-by-step approach to gain freedom from addiction to drugs or alcohol or any other compulsive behavior makes sense just on the face of it. Compulsive behavior is not likely to go away overnight. Overcoming can be a long, difficult process, and it makes a great deal of sense to move toward victory one small step at a time, instead of trying to change your life immediately—everything all at once.

In recent years, the Twelve Steps have been modified for use by churches and other Christian organizations to make them of better use to believers. Now, the Twelve Steps have always been "religious." They have always referred to a higher power, a spiritual awakening. But in order to be as accessible as possible, and thus useful to as many people as possible, no reference was ever made to Christ. (It is worth noting, though, that even though the preeminence of Christ is not mentioned in the Twelve Steps, there is a recognition of the existence and importance of the spiritual dimension in achieving recovery from compulsive behavior.)

For the purposes of this book, we will use a modified version of the Twelve Steps, which *does* acknowledge Christ's power and willingness to help us accomplish the steps. Before we begin talking about the steps themselves, I need to mention that every one of them must be experienced, and not merely assented to on an intellectual basis. Each step in succession involves things that *must* be done in order to bring about recovery, and each step must be dealt with fully before you can move on to the next one.

As we begin looking at the steps one by one, you might see that you have already completed one or more of them. If so, fine—as long as you take the time to really consider the matter and *make sure* you have done everything the step requires of you.

Perhaps you will find that for you, some of the steps will be accomplished quite easily. If so, that's terrific.

But there are some steps that will undoubtedly take time and effort. You will have to do some soul-searching, some digging around down in what are probably some painful areas of your soul, in order to uncover your true motivations and feelings. You will almost certainly have to dredge up some matters that you would just as soon leave buried. You are probably going to have to seek out some people that you'd much rather leave alone. But all of this is necessary to achieve wholeness.

Remember, before we get into them too deeply, that a superficial rushing through of the Twelve Steps will not produce the desired recovery—and recovery is what we are after.

Although most of the steps also require introspection—looking within and learning something about yourself—they have to do with the self as it relates first of all to God, and then to others.

In this chapter, we will discuss the first three steps—steps that have to do for the most part with looking to God. Then, in chapter 9, we will discuss steps four through seven, which have to do with the (sometimes rather unpleasant) task of self-examination. Finally, in chapter 10, we will move on to steps eight through twelve, which have to do with looking to others.

Here are the first three of the Twelve Steps:

1. I admitted that I was powerless over my particular compulsion, and that my life had become unmanageable.
2. I came to believe that a power greater than myself could restore me to sanity.
3. I made a decision to turn my will and my life over to God.

Now let's take them one at a time:

First, Step Number One: *I admitted that I was powerless over my particular compulsion, and that my life had become unmanageable.*

"My sins have overtaken me" (Psalm 40:12).

Upon first reading, this step seems simple enough. But it may not be. I have known men who have struggled for months to accomplish it. They wanted to admit they were powerless—but they didn't really think it was true. They had tremendous difficulty getting to the point where they weren't trying to do things in their own power—and where they could admit that their lives had become unmanageable.

But the beginning of the journey toward spiritual wholeness is the admission that you have a problem. All future progress and avoidance of relapse is founded on the successful completion of the first step. For men who have been taught that they always have to be in charge of every aspect of their lives, admitting that they truly have no power at all over something or other is an extremely difficult thing to do.

Men are raised to believe that only sissies have weaknesses. A man may think he has *a few* weaknesses, but he certainly doesn't want anyone else to know about them.

It's also hard for men in general to admit that things are beyond their control. For men with compulsive personalities, it goes beyond "hard" and becomes "nearly impossible." This man can be very controlling of himself, and others, too, and he can be reluctant to give up something that seems to be such a big part of his manliness.

Yet the Scriptures promise us that "God gives grace to the humble but opposes the proud."[1] Admitting powerlessness is an indication that the stubborn male pride is being humbled—and that, in turn, means that you are closer to attaining a special measure of grace from God.

The way to get help from above is not trying harder, *per se*, but rather surrendering—letting go of things and allowing God to come in and change you.

By "trying harder" a compulsive person can sometimes stop his troubling behavior for a short period of time. But it is not likely to last. Actually, as we discussed when we talked about recovery from alcoholism, this sort of "stopping-by-willpower" is actually dangerous, because it can produce an illusory sense of being in control. Unfortunately, the truly compulsive will almost always eventually return to his compulsion.

This is like the story of "The Little Engine That Could," only it's in reverse. You remember that story from your childhood: The little engine huffs and puffs as it makes its way up the hill, "I think I can . . . I think I can," and sure enough, it succeeds. That's the sort of image we've all grown up with. We tend to think we can grit our teeth, roll up our sleeves, and get the task done. But for the person who is trapped in compulsive behavior, there is a time when he has to look at his life and realize that from where he is right now, he may be, "The little engine who *can't*." He's just not going to make it if he relies on his own power. He needs help!

The paradox of this first step is that, in order to gain victory, you must give up control.

It's just like Jesus said in Matthew 10:39: "Whoever finds his life will lose it, and whoever loses his life for my sake will find it."

If you can let go of the control, and admit that you need help, you will find that Help is waiting.

Attend any meeting of AA, and you will hear those in attendance introduce themselves by saying, "My name is _____and I am an alcoholic." Why do they do that? Because the admission that "I am an alcoholic" is also the admission that "I recognize myself for what I am. I have an addiction, and I am powerless in the face of that addiction."

It's necessary to mention here that powerlessness against a compulsive behavior may not translate into powerlessness and helplessness in other areas of life. You may appear to others to be quite strong. You may appear to yourself to be quite strong. Except in that one particular area of life.

As Peter Trachtenberg notes, "Many addicts and alcoholics are at least superficially successful and effective individuals. . . . Indeed, what impresses anyone who studies such personalities is the radical split between their outer and inner selves, the one assertive, elastic, and assured, the other frail, insecure, and fearful."[2]

Truthfully, admitting your lack of power and control is more than a one-time thing. It's something that needs to be done over and over, every time you feel tempted to take matters back into your own hands, and to try to change your life by and through your own power.

I'm sure you've heard the old joke about the prize-fighter who's taking a savage beating at the hands of his bigger, stronger opponent: As he comes back to his corner after a round in which he has been particularly bloodied and bruised, his trainer says, "You're doing great! He never laid a glove on you!"

To which, the fighter replies, "If he hasn't laid a glove on me, you'd better keep your eye on the referee—because somebody's beating the daylights out of me!"

Like that fighter, a person who is going to try to overcome compulsive behavior by his own power is going to be badly beaten. He's likely to get knocked down time and time again. It won't matter how often he denies that it's happening, or insists that he's going to do better next time. Until he comes to the end of himself, admits his own powerlessness, and faces up to the fact that he needs help, very little is likely to change.

Step Number Two: *I came to believe that a power greater than myself could restore me to sanity.*

"We believe and know that you are the Holy One of God" (John 6:69).

Realizing that self-will is not going to produce the lasting changes that need to occur in your life is a big step, primarily because it enables you to realize that you have to look to someone else for help.

For the Christian (and, actually, for the non-Christian, too) there is only one Person to turn to for this help, and that is God. As you begin to grow in awareness of your own powerlessness to change your life, so should you begin to grow in your awareness that God *does* have the power to change your life, and that He is ready and willing to do so.

"Coming to believe" is a process that lifts the addict out of the pit of despair and onto a foundation of hope. It makes him realize that real hope comes only from God.

Maybe you already have a strong belief in God. If you do, much of what I say over the next few pages may seem very basic. You may find yourself thinking, "I already know all that." But surprisingly enough, there are thousands upon thousands of people who don't know or understand these first principles of the Christian faith, and who honestly have no idea that God is able or willing to change their lives. And remember, too, that we have to lay the foundation before we can begin to build on it. Intellectual assent is no substitute for experiencing the reality of an honest relationship with Jesus.

For the compulsive, the object of his lust—whatever that may be—has been his god for years. It is now time for him to focus his attention on the real God, the Lord of heaven and earth.

While I was working in a secular drug and alcohol rehabilitation center, this step enabled me to present the gospel to many recovering addicts and lead them to Christ. Christ can and does change lives.

Where people have trouble with this step—even many Christians—is that they believe that God *can* restore them, but they're not too sure that He *wants* to restore them.

But the good news is that He *does* want to. He's not only ready to help you, He's eager to help you. In fact, that's what the gospel is all about.

Jesus Christ's death, burial, and resurrection is a dramatic indication of God's desire to restore people to sanity. Mankind in general had turned its collective back on God, and had become separated from Him. And when that happened, *He* was the one who took steps to make things right. That's why Jesus Christ walked this earth in human form for thirty-three years, experiencing all the pain and anguish that life on this planet entails. He was calling men and women everywhere to be restored.

But even then, most people weren't interested in being restored. They proved that, first of all by ignoring His message, and then by turning on Him and murdering Him.

And even on the cross, Christ still expressed love and forgiveness for those who were killing Him. There could be no greater expression of God's love.

But if you're still one of those who has trouble believing that God would want to help you, then I refer you to Luke

15 and the parable of the prodigal son. Keep in mind that the father in this story is representative of our heavenly Father, and that this is the story of every man who realizes he has failed God miserably:

"But while he was still a long way off, his father saw him and was filled with compassion for him; he ran to his son, threw his arms around him and kissed him" (verse 20).

God isn't the type of Father who waits for us to come to Him on our hands and knees to ask for something, and then glowers down at us, "Well, what do you want now?" He is not the type of Father, even, who is willing to meet us halfway. He is the type who runs, as fast as He can, to meet us, the first moment He sees any indication on our part that we have come to the realization that we need His help.

The Bible is full of this type of imagery.

God is the Good Shepherd who will go to any length to rescue one lost sheep, even though there are ninety-nine other sheep safely in the fold.

He is the one who says, "Come to me, all you who are weary and burdened, and I will give you rest. Take my yoke upon you and learn from me, for I am gentle and humble in heart, and you will find rest for your souls. For my yoke is easy and my burden is light."[3]

Step Number Three: *I made a decision to turn my will and my life over to God.*

"Everyone who calls upon the name of the Lord will be saved" (Romans 10:13).

This necessary step—and really it's a necessary step for *everyone*—is a particularly difficult one for a compulsive person to take. I say that this step is necessary for everyone because it is only through surrender to God that you can come into His kingdom; only through acknowledging Jesus Christ as "Lord and Savior" that salvation is obtained.

Surrender to God begins with a person kneeling before God and praying something along the lines of, "Holy Father, I realize that I am a sinner . . . and that Jesus Christ suffered on the cross as atonement for my sins. I believe that He died, was buried, but rose from the dead—and that through my faith in Him, and His atoning sacrifice, I will be able to live with you throughout eternity. I acknowledge Him as the Lord and Savior of my life."

Or you can just pray—"Jesus, help!"

That is the very important place where surrender begins. But it goes far beyond that, too. Surrender involves getting to the point where you truly want to have every aspect of your life under the Lord's control. I say "want to have" because that's the key. Few of us can actually ever get to the point where we can say that we're fully surrendered to God's will. But as things come up in our lives that are obviously *not* surrendered, we have opportunity to take them to Him in prayer. In other words, surrender to God's will is likely going to be a long-term, continuous process. But Step Three has been completed when you have told Him that you want Him to take control of your life, and you have acknowledged your utter dependence upon Christ for salvation.

An addictions counselor once said to me, "You can't say no to an addict. They want their own way."

That's true, but in order for him to achieve wholeness, the addicted person must stop demanding his own way. He has to quit trying to manipulate and control others and surrender His own will to God.

And if you're having difficulty surrendering, you need to understand that surrender doesn't necessarily have to be painful. In this instance, to surrender means that you stop struggling and fighting, and come to God so He can give you that "rest for your soul" that Jesus talks about in the eleventh chapter of Matthew.

It wasn't too long ago that American soldiers were fighting a war in the deserts of the Middle East: You may remember, how, during one part of Operation Desert Storm, hundreds and perhaps even thousands of Iraqi troops were coming as fast as they could to surrender to the allied forces. The strange thing about it was that they weren't coming with heads hung low, as if they were doing something that was distasteful and painful. They were surren-

114 / Three Compulsions That Defeat Most Men

dering with heads held high. Some of them were actually running toward the allied troops. It was almost as if they just couldn't surrender fast enough. Any outside observer would have thought they were being liberated—and, sure enough they were.

You see . . . surrender *is* sometimes the same thing as liberation.

Have you ever truly surrendered your life to God? Are you sure you have?

Some people are able to yield to God without a struggle, but that's rare. Others have quite a battle with it, and are always having to ask Him for His help, and there's nothing wrong with that.

But remember . . . it all starts with a heartfelt cry: "Lord, I give up! I surrender!"

Only through surrender can you achieve ultimate victory. And only when you understand that your loving, forgiving Father is in charge of your life can you move on to the task that lies ahead.

Are you ready? It's time to turn the spotlight on yourself.

9
LOOKING TO SELF

In the previous chapter, we recognized and admitted our own powerlessness. Then we turned our attention to God's power and might, realizing that it is only through Him that we can become whole and spiritually mature. Finally, we appropriated God's power for our lives by making a conscious decision to surrender *our* wills to *His* will.

Over these first three steps, we've come to some important realizations and made some very important decisions.

Now it's time to begin taking the steps that will produce in us the growth and maturity we seek.

But in order to grow, we have to take a long, hard look at ourselves, and make some changes in our lives. For that reason, these next four steps are often among the most difficult ones to take.

It is never easy for an honest man to look at himself. That's because if he is honest, he'll have to admit all of the times he's failed, and all of the wrong things he's done.

Reality is that all of us, without exception, have many things hidden away that we really wouldn't want anyone else to know about; things that we've tried to forget about ourselves.

But now comes the time when we have to deal with all these skeletons in our closets—all the shadowy things that we wish we hadn't done—but can't take back.

It is not easy by any stretch of the imagination, but anyone who wants to grow has to face up to the deeper issues of his life—he has to confront the shadows.

Steps four through seven are:

4. I made a searching and fearless moral inventory of myself.
5. I admitted to God, to myself, and to another human being the exact nature of my wrongs.
6. I became entirely ready to have God remove all of these defects from my character.
7. I humbly asked God to remove my shortcomings.

Let's move on into Step Number Four: *I made a searching and fearless moral inventory of myself.*

"Search me, O God, and know my heart; see if there is any offensive way in me" (Psalm 139:23).

This is the only one of the first seven of the Twelve Steps that does not directly involve looking to God. Instead, it involves looking within . . . but it is God-oriented because it can only be done with God's help, and it is preparation for asking God to make some major changes in your life.

Self-examination is a hard thing for many men to do. That's because their whole focus has been on objects external to themselves, which they can use to fill their inner emptiness. The typically defensive and manipulative compulsive male will especially resist any introspection, because it might force him to see himself clearly.

Compulsive types tend to hurt other people by their behavior. They hurt their spouses, their parents, their children, and any others who will let them get away with it. They behave immorally. No wonder they don't want to look inside themselves and take note of what they see. It's not likely to be a very pretty sight! But this is exactly what you have to do to complete Step Number Four.

When clients who are compulsive come to me for counseling, I have them write out a complete "addictions history." I ask the drinkers and drug-users to write about the first time they ever got high, and about every time after that—as many times as they can remember.

I ask the person who is addicted to sex to write a complete sexual history. The purpose of this exercise is that it helps the client to see clearly the reality of his dysfunctional and sinful ways. Once he has seen, written down in "black and white," some of the things he has done, he is no longer able to deny that he has a problem. He has to face up to the fact that, "Yeah, I really need help in this area."

Another reason this step can be very difficult for the compulsive man is that he is generally filled with a free-floating sense of guilt anyway. But whereas a nebulous feeling of unease and guilt will not be of benefit to anyone, genuine guilt, over genuinely wrong acts, can lead to godly sorrow and repentance, which, in turn, can lead to forgiveness and freedom.

How deep does Step Four go? Very deep.

And although I wouldn't go so far as to suggest that you write a book about all of your misdeeds, I do believe that you should spend some time really going over your life, and writing down the things you see—particularly the ways you have failed, and the ways in which you would like to be a better person.

Have you ever stolen anything, or hurt people by lying to them, or cheated on your spouse? Put it on your list.

Do you recognize that you tend to be irresponsible, that others just can't count on you? That goes on your list, too.

Do you hide from reality by drinking or using drugs?

Don't just write, "I tend to be irresponsible," or "I tend to hide from reality by drinking alcohol." You need to get down to specifics, like: "I promised my son Bobby that I would be at his junior-high-school talent show, and I didn't show up. He was hurt and angry, and had every right to be."

You really have to get down to the minute details if you're really going to face up to and deal with your problems.

When it comes to preparing your "fearless moral inventory," I would suggest that you take an entire day—or even a weekend. Go some place where you know you won't be disturbed, and spend as much time as possible thinking about your life. Ask God to help you, to shine His spotlight on things that you might have forgotten—or tried to forget—that you really need to see. If you're really open to it, He'll do what you ask of Him. It might be painful—but the pain is necessary for growth.

Someone says, "But I don't want to see all these things about myself. It will just make me feel like a failure."

Let me tell you something about failures:

- Winston Churchill was considered to be washed-up after he made critical tactical mistakes during World War I.
- Louis Pasteur received the lowest grade in his chemistry class.
- A producer told Lucille Ball to give up acting because she wasn't any good at it.
- A publisher told Zane Grey to "quit wasting our time" with novels because "you can't write."
- Albert Einstein got poor grades in school.
- And . . . the biggest shocker of all, the apostle Peter—the man who was so instrumental in the spread of Christianity in the first century—denied Christ not once or twice . . . but *three times.*

All of these men and women failed at one time or another, or were considered to be failures by their peers. But instead of giving up, they all examined themselves, resolved that they would all do better next time. And, with God's help, all of them *did* do better next time.

Past failure must be seen as the stepping-stone to present and future success.

Don't look back and say, "Well, I failed before, so I'm bound to fail again." Instead, say, "I failed before, but I see why now."

Once you have completed your "searching and fearless moral inventory," it is time to move on to Step Number Five: *I admitted to God, myself, and another human being the exact nature of my wrongs.*

"Confess your sins one to another, that you may be healed" (James 5:16).

That scripture verse gives the idea behind the fifth step. A proud man has great difficulty admitting when he is wrong, and a great deal of pride is usually found among men who are actively engaged in their addiction. For the recovering man, however, humility must take the place of pride, and repentance must replace sin.

Admitting our sins to God is the first step in establishing a relationship with Him through Jesus. Our wrongs, our mistakes, and our sins must be admitted, confessed, and faced. The compulsive man denies his sin, and also denies how his addiction may be hurting those who love him.

Admitting your wrongs to yourself is also an important part of breaking the denial so commonly found among compulsive types. The great Reformer John Calvin said that knowledge of one's self leads to knowledge of God. You have to know and accept the truth about yourself, as painful as that truth may be, before you can achieve wholeness.

Admitting to another human being the exact nature of our wrongs brings us into an honest relationship. It is also the hardest part of Step Number Five. After all, even though you are admitting to God what you've done, you know that He isn't shocked or surprised, because He has really known about it all along. And even though facing up to what you've done may be difficult for you, it's not as if you're telling any secrets about yourself.

But when it comes to admitting to another person what you've done . . . that *is* telling secrets, and you may feel that you're running the risk of him thinking that you're a really bad person.

Besides that, opening up to another person in that way makes you vulnerable . . . and that's a very uneasy feeling for the compulsive type, because it involves the risk of being rejected. Many compulsive men are very mistrustful of people. They learned early in life not to depend on or trust other men, and so they have become isolated and have few, if any, close friends. It takes trust to admit "the exact nature of your wrongs" to another human being—and that's precisely what this step requires: trust.

A warning is in order, though. I am not suggesting that you grab just anyone and talk to him about all the sins you've committed. It's bad when you don't trust anyone, but it can be worse if you think you can trust everyone. You must be selective. The other person has to be someone whom you know to be responsible, reliable, and capable of keeping things in confidence. Whom can you trust with your confession? Your pastor perhaps, or a professional therapist, or your sponsor in a group (such as Alcoholics Anonymous). It can be a friend, but it needs to be a friend in whom you have confidence, that you really feel you can trust.

Blessed is the man who has a trusted confidant with whom he can share his struggles, confess his sins, and who will hold him accountable for his behavior. Too few men have a spiritual confessor or counselor.

It should *not* be your spouse, however. Your spouse should not become your mother or your spiritual confessor. This will damage the relationship just as badly as the compulsive behavior did in the first place. Allowing a spouse to become something that she was never intended to be is foolish.

For the Christian, confessing one's sins to another should be followed by the confessor declaring aloud, "Jesus Christ forgives your sin." This declaration of forgiveness is very healing, can be made by a friend or pastor, and there is nothing at all presumptuous about it, because, as the Bible says in 1 John 1:9: "If we confess our sins, He is faithful and just and will forgive us our sins and purify us from all unrighteousness."

Many men have a great deal of trouble believing this. They struggle with forgiving themselves, so they think that God won't forgive them either.

But the Bible is full of references to God's love and forgiveness.

For example, Psalm 103:12: "As far as the east is from the west, so far has he removed our transgressions from us."

And Micah 7:19: "You will again have compassion on us; you will tread our sins underfoot and hurl all our iniquities into the depths of the sea."

In other words, not only is God willing to forgive—but when He does, He puts our sins so far away from Him that it's as if they never really happened.

That's why we are told in Hebrews 4:16 that we can "approach the throne of grace with confidence, so that we may receive mercy and find grace to help us in our time of need."

The Bible contains dozens of verses like these, and reading them on a regular basis—or even memorizing some of them—will help you gain the confidence you need to complete Step Number Five.

Once that Step is completed, you are ready for Step Number Six, which is: *I became entirely ready to have God remove all these defects from my character.*

This is another step that sounds easier than it may really be.

Why wouldn't anyone want God to remove the defects from his character? Because he may enjoy those defects. He may enjoy getting drunk or high, or sleeping with anyone who will sleep with him.

Do you really want to be set free from the compulsions that bind you? Until you do want your freedom, you're not likely to change, and life is going to go on being a struggle.

The point of Step Six is to refocus on God and your need of Him. It is a reaffirmation of what we now know—that only He can change us. Our puny attempts at self-improvement fall short of the transformation that the Holy Spirit seeks to accomplish in us.

All that is required in this step is to be ready for the Holy Spirit to do His work in our lives. As the recovering man begins to see himself more clearly, he will also notice that many areas of his life need adjustment and correction. He will see that along with his compulsions he may be overly critical, insensitive to others, or withdrawn and aloof. He may find that his spouse has legitimate complaints about things such as his unwillingness to share household chores, his inability to communicate, or his tendency to be moody or irritable.

He may have difficulty trusting authority figures or allowing others to get close to him. The list of areas where he needs to change may be quite lengthy, but the important thing right now is that he becomes willing to let go in all of these areas, no matter how many there are.

Again, in this step, you don't have to *do* anything at all. You just have to get to the point where you're willing to *let God* do something.

Can you honestly say that you have made yourself ready for God to remove all of your character defects? Do you want God to help you to be willing to change?

If so, then it's time to move on to Step Number Seven: *I humbly asked God to remove my shortcomings.*

"Jesus looked at them and said, 'With man this is impossible, but not with God; all things are possible with God' " (Mark 10:27).

Far too many men find themselves stuck in the quicksand of a lifestyle that is sucking them down to destruction. They feel unable to change, despite all of the many promises they've made to others that they *will* change.

There is only one way these men are going to be able to honor their promises; one answer to the predicament in which they find themselves: asking God for help!

I once worked with a client who harbored a great deal of resentment toward his boss, and who was using this resentment as an excuse for his drinking. The man was a Christian, so I encouraged him to pray for his boss's well-being. He didn't want to do it at first, but finally agreed that he would, because he couldn't escape the fact that Jesus told us to pray for our enemies.

As he began to pray for his boss, something happened. He felt his resentment and anger beginning to melt away, slowly. In time he developed a new understanding for the man. And as he did, another excuse to get drunk fell by the wayside, and my client's recovery was strengthened.

Asking God to remove all of your shortcomings is more—much more—than praying a simple prayer: "Dear God, please remove all my shortcomings. Thank you. Amen."

It involves looking at all those character defects you uncovered during the compilation of your "fearless moral inventory" and taking them before God one at a time—"doing battle" in prayer as you seek to be set free.

What gives you the most trouble in your life? Which behavior would you most like to change? Start now, asking God to remove that character defect from your life and change you. Remember, the most important aspect of this prayer is the new honesty you are developing with God.

Most often when we think of a shortcoming, we think of things we do that we know are sinful. Yet, it is also a shortcoming to become obsessed with our own performance and the performance of others. We know we are saved by grace, but deep down we fear that we have to follow a law to make us truly righteous. The only trouble is that this law changes based on what your faith group sees as important. The end result is that we can become very legalistic and see our relationship to God in terms of what we do, not on who we are in Christ. We strive to feel good about ourselves as Christians by doing more. This leads to a sense of spiritual pride, or conversely, it can lead to feeling defeated, like we can never measure up.

The biggest shortcoming we could have is failing to enter into His rest. It is time to rest from our works and receive the peace and grace that only Jesus can bring us. That's the Good News of Christ's love!

Change is probably not going to come in the flash of an instant—one moment you're a workaholic and the next moment you're not—but as you continue to pray and seek God in the matter, I am confident that you will see continued improvement.

Sometimes we human beings tend to be extremely impatient. We want God to act "right now." But He has all eternity in mind, and He always acts according to what is best for us over the long-term.

Surrendering to and seeking God's will above your own is the wisest way to pray. If we can submit to what the Holy Spirit is calling us to, we will experience the serenity that He brings. Our nature is to want what we want when we want it, but wisdom tells us to say yes to Jesus and yield to His love.

The next part of the journey involves "looking to others." And that's what we will be doing in the last five of these Twelve Steps.

10
LOOKING TO OTHERS

The compulsive person isn't likely to have very many friends.

In fact he may not have *any* close friends, people with whom he can let his guard down and share on an intimate basis.

Now it's time to work on changing that.

So far, we've looked upward . . . and then inward . . . and now it's time to look outward.

In other words, we started off on our journey through the Twelve Steps by taking a long, hard look at ourselves. Then we talked about improving our relationship with God, and about learning to look to Him as the source of help in overcoming compulsive, damaging behavior. In this chapter we're going to complete our journey through the Twelve Steps—first of all, by seeking to improve our relationships with others.

The last of Twelve Steps are:

8. I made a list of all the people I had harmed, and became willing to make amends to them all.
9. I made direct amends to such people wherever possible, except when to do so would injure them or others.
10. I continued to take personal inventory, and when I was wrong, promptly admitted it.
11. I sought through prayer and meditation to improve my conscious contact with God, praying only for knowledge of His will for me and the power to carry that out.
12. Having had a spiritual awakening as a result of

these steps, I tried to carry this message to others, and to practice these principles in all my affairs.

We've talked about the parable of the prodigal son before, but whenever I think of the compulsive person's relationships with others, my mind just naturally goes back to the protagonist of this parable.

The prodigal son was a first-century "Good-Time Charlie" who seemed to have plenty of friends just as long as he had plenty of money. While he was supplying the booze and the dope, everyone thought he was a great guy. But their admiration for him extended no further than the bottom line in his bank account.

As soon as the money ran out, they all deserted him like rats abandoning a sinking ship. There wasn't one person who really cared. No one he could turn to in his time of trouble. Not one *true* friend.

As he was left to contemplate the emptiness of his life, it must have come home to him how these people had just been using him to get what they wanted. In turn, the realization would undoubtedly have led him to see how he had done the same thing.

Well, of course, the parable of the prodigal son has a happy ending. The young man came to his senses, and was restored to his father and his family. Thankfully, the same thing can happen to the compulsive person who has alienated others by his behavior—who has cut himself off even from those who really do (or did) care about him.

It doesn't matter what your interpersonal relationships have been like up to this point, it *is* possible for you to have decent, mutually respectful relationships with other people.

It's going to take work on your part, but it's going to prove more than worth the effort you expend.

The first item of business on your "healing-of-relationships" agenda is Step Number Eight: *I made a list of all those I had harmed, and became willing to make amends to them all.*

"Go and be reconciled to your brother" (Matthew 5:24).

Like the prodigal son, the compulsive man often leaves a trail of offended relationships. The task, in this step, is to make a list of all those who have been harmed by your behavior, and then to *become willing* to make amends to them. Not to make amends, but to be *willing* to make amends.

For the compulsive person, the relationship he has with his work, his bottle, or his sexual fantasies can be more important than the relationships he has with people. If you want to know how deeply someone is "into" his compulsion, take a look at his interpersonal relationships. Generally it is true that the worse those relationships are, the tighter the grip of the compulsion.

What are some of the offenses for which you might need to make amends?

Perhaps you have to acknowledge that your priorities have been wrong, and that you have neglected your family as a result. By the time you have completed this step, you should be willing to apologize to your spouse and/or children for your past behavior, and make amends by demonstrating a changed attitude.

You may have to apologize to your wife for "ogling" other women, or being flirtatious, and you can make amends by not doing that sort of thing any longer.

Did you damage a relationship with a friend by lying to him about something? That, too, is something that merits an apology.

Perhaps you hurt someone in a dating relationship, misrepresenting your feelings for someone in order to get her to give in to you sexually. That, too, is an area where an apology is warranted.

In other words, anything you have done to hurt someone, any time you have used someone, Step Eight requires that you make yourself willing to make things right. Generally, you can use the personal inventory you prepared in Step Four to help you carry out Step Eight.

Again, ask the Lord to help you remember those events about which you need to make amends, and those people to whom you must apologize. As those people and events come to mind, ask Him to melt your heart and make you willing to do the right thing.

And, then, it's time for the hard part of putting Step Eight into practice. Because, as you have undoubtedly already figured out, Step Number Nine is: *I made direct amends to such people wherever possible.*

Ouch! Apologizing is always a hard thing to do, to go to someone and say, "I really behaved badly toward you and I'm sorry. Will you please forgive me?" Human pride doesn't handle that sort of thing very well. But making direct amends to people who have suffered due to your insensitivity is a demonstration of your sincerity.

Yet, in light of the compulsive's history of selfishness, this step also warns that, in the name of recovery, indiscreet actions can also harm others. For instance, a sexually compulsive man in recovery may think he should go and apologize to the husband of a woman with whom he has slept. Obviously, this would harm a marriage that may be quite shaky already. In a situation like this, it would be far better to make amends by refraining from such behavior in the future.

Or suppose you had always been "using" someone who considers you to be a good friend—who has never expected that you were only being nice to him in order to indulge your compulsion. You would be doing absolutely no good, and probably quite a bit of harm, if you went to him and said, "Joe, I want you to know that I've never really been your friend. I've only been using you all these years, and I'm really sorry about that."

Joe is not going to be happy that you came to apologize. He is going to be devastated. It would be far better to resolve that from now on you would *not* be a user, and that you would seek to be a true friend to Joe.

What I am saying, then, is that good judgment and discretion are absolutely essential for the proper carrying out of Step Nine.

I remember Tommy, who had always been extremely attracted to women. After he got married, his interest in other women didn't decline. His wife often caught him looking at them—actually, "leering" is more the correct word—and she was hurt and belittled by his actions.

After he acknowledged and dealt with his lustful behavior, Tommy sought to make amends to his wife by building her up. By complimenting her and being attentive to her and asking her advice on matters both large and small, he showed her that he really wanted to love her in a way that she would appreciate.

Not only had he stopped his hurtful behavior, but he was showing his wife that he truly valued her, not only as a woman, but as a human being.

I am sometimes asked, "What can I do if the person I offended has died?"

In that situation, I suggest writing a letter of apology. Doing so is a good way to free yourself from the sharply focused guilt you may now be feeling—since you are becoming more aware of the things you have done and the ways you have hurt people. It might even be helpful to write yourself a letter from the offended party, expressing their forgiveness.

If the person is deceased, and thus cannot accept your apology, writing it out yourself, on their behalf, is a good way to bring closure to the subject.

I have also been asked, "What if I need to make restitution?"

If you've hurt someone financially, if you've stolen from him, or cheated him in some way, then yes, by all means, make restitution.

You need to wipe the slate completely clean so you can start over . . . and leaving unpaid debts hanging in the air is not a good way to start over.

Another question that comes up: "Do I have to apologize in person?"

No, not at all. If you can sit down with the person, face-to-face, then I'd recommend it. A face-to-face meeting adds emphasis to your apology. It can mean a lot to the offended party that you cared enough to come by in person and try to set things straight.

But sometimes a face-to-face meeting can be awkward, or strained, or impossible when you live many miles away from the person you offended.

In any situation, there is nothing at all wrong with making a phone call, or writing a letter. In fact, writing a letter can be the very best way to apologize, because it gives you a chance to say everything you need and want to say. In the nervousness of a face-to-face meeting or telephone call, important things may be left unsaid. But if you write a letter, you can always rewrite, edit, and change things until you say exactly what you want to say.

One final point: What if the person won't forgive you?

The only thing to be said about that is that it's not your problem. You have no control over the other person's attitude or feelings, and if he won't forgive you, you at least have the satisfaction of knowing that you have tried to make amends. And that's all this step asks of you.

I'm not saying that you shouldn't try again to get the offended party to accept your apology. But if, after several tries on your part, the person still won't forgive you, then stop struggling and rest in the fact that you have behaved in a way that is proper, and pleasing to God.

Now we move on to Step Number Ten, which is: *I continued to take personal inventory, and when I was wrong promptly admitted it.*

"Father, I have sinned against heaven and you" (Luke 15:18).

This step has to do with taking the garbage out on a daily basis.

If you've ever forgotten to take the garbage out, you know how quickly it can accumulate. What's more, if you've ever forgotten to take it out for more than a couple of days, you know how it can start to stink.

Really, that's what has happened to the compulsive person. His life has become full of garbage, which has caused a terrible smell. Taking a personal inventory on a regular basis, and dealing with issues as they come up is a good way to prevent a recurrence.

First John 1:8 says, "If we say that we have no sin, we deceive ourselves, and the truth is not in us."

That sounds kind of harsh, I realize, but it's more than an indictment of human nature. It is also an acknowledgement that nobody is perfect.

This is a very good verse to keep in mind as you continue to grow spiritually. For remember, spiritual maturity is not so much a destination as it is a journey and a way of life.

The important thing is to deal with whatever setbacks you may see *right now* while they are still fresh in your mind. You can deal with them by:

- Acknowledging them to God, asking His forgiveness, and His help so that you don't stumble again.
- Immediately apologizing to those you might have offended by your actions, thus keeping your slate as clean as possible, and letting others know that you really are striving to change.
- Analyzing the situation to see if there was some particular thing that caused you to fail that can be avoided in the future.

If you carefully look things over, you may see that your moments of stumbling are tied to a particular person, place, or activity. Is there someone you really ought to avoid because he always gets you involved in your compulsion? Then stay away from him. Is there some place where your compulsion is particularly in evidence? Then avoid that place.

The recovering alcoholic who thinks he can hang out with the guys at the pub is playing with fire. He may insist that he's just going in to play a couple of games of darts, or to watch the football game on television, but his old surroundings and his old friends are likely to bring him down.

In his book *Getting Over Getting High*, Bernard Green says, "I stress over and over again that social changes need to accompany the physical stopping of stimulants, especially for the young."[1]

Please remember that it is not a sin to be tempted. We are all human, and the Scriptures tell us that Jesus was tempted in the same way we are.[2] You can't avoid temptation altogether, but you *can* avoid running headlong toward it.

After all, the Lord's Prayer says, "Lead us not into temptation."[3] We all need to avoid temptation as much as we possibly can. Being tempted does not mean you are sinning, nor does it mean that you lack discipline. It simply means that you are human.

And, like all humans, you have a great need for God to be involved in your life. That brings us to Step Number Eleven: *I sought through prayer and meditation to improve my conscious contact with God, praying only for knowledge of His will for me and the power to carry that out.*

"May your will be done" (Matthew 26:24).

This is another very big step for the compulsive man who has, in the past, used substances, people, or experiences to escape the pain buried deep within himself. Now, this step calls for him to look within himself to find the kingdom of God.

It requires quiet time alone, reading the Bible, and other Christian books or devotionals; and it requires growing in relationships with other men with whom you can be honest.

Part of this step involves praying for the knowledge of His will for your life and for the power to carry it out.

In *Don't Call It Love*, Patrick Carnes has several excellent suggestions designed to help the compulsive person strengthen his spiritual life.[4] Among them are:

- Use the Twelve Steps. They are a proven recipe for spiritual wholeness. Remember that the program started with the realization that without the spiritual component, recovery could not happen. Decide a spiritual life is essential, not an option.
- Find guides. Listen to others share their spiritual experiences and ask how healing happened in their lives.
- Separate religion from spirituality. Many come with "baggage" about religious institutions that damaged or constricted their growth. Resentment about these experiences can cast shadows over genuine spiritual development.
- Connect with nature. Spirituality starts with a sense

of marvel at our existence and at the wonders of creation—other living things, the oceans and mountains, forests, deserts, and weather. Go for a walk. Watch stars. Take care of a pet. Notice your body. Play with children. Then connect these miracles with what else you see around you.

- Make a daily effort. Key to spiritual life is constancy. Daily rituals that anchor your sense of stability help you to achieve incremental spiritual growth. Then when leaps of faith are required and stress overwhelms you, a reservoir of accumulated strength awaits.
- Surrender. All inner journeys start with an "emptying of self." Serenity, according to the prayer, is doing all you can and accepting that that is enough.

Always remember, God loves you! He wants only the best for you! And for those reasons, any time you invest in seeking to uncover God's will for your life will be time very well spent! It's very unfortunate that so many Christian parents have done such a poor job of presenting God's love to their children. So many times it seems that they have tried to use God's wrath to scare their children into being good, but it has had the exact opposite effect from what was intended.

And now we come to the final step—Step Number Twelve: *Having had a spiritual awakening as a result of these steps, I tried to carry this message to others, and to practice these principles in all my affairs.*

"Return home and tell how much God has done for you" (Luke 8:39).

One of the things that we all want to do whenever something wonderful happens to us is to tell our friends and families about it.

If Ed McMahon suddenly showed up on your doorstep with a check for ten million dollars, would you say, "Shhh! Be careful! The neighbors might see you!"

I don't think so. You would just naturally want others to share in your good fortune and celebrate with you.

And that's what this final step is all about: carrying the good news to others so that they, too, might benefit from God's grace and power as administered through the Twelve Steps.

The sad fact is that there are millions of men (and women, too) trapped in compulsive behavior, and all of them need to be set free. They need to know what you have discovered—that there is a way of escape. They need to know that God is alive and well and that He cares for them. They need to experience the same type of spiritual renewal that you have experienced.

The emphasis on seeking God's will and examining oneself for sinful behavior will produce growth in a man who had previously shut God and others out of his life by his destructive behavior. A man who really experiences the Twelve Steps will naturally be able to help others, and that help will come primarily through sharing how the steps have helped him—or, more precisely, how God has worked through the steps to help him.

I am not suggesting that you go door-to-door to tell strangers about what has happened in your life. But I am suggesting that the person who has been set free in this way should always be ready, when the occasion arises, to spread the message that there is hope and that wholeness is possible.

Not long ago I read the testimony of a man who was once a terrible alcoholic. He achieved sobriety through a Twelve-Step program back in 1950. For several years prior to sobriety, booze had been the single most important thing in this man's life. But now he has not touched a drop of alcohol for more than forty years! Change *is* possible; lasting, life-enhancing change.

So always be ready to share the good news of the possibility of abundant life. There are lives in need of saving.

In my view, the two most important aspects of the Twelve Steps are:

1. An acknowledgement that self-will alone cannot overcome man's sinful nature.

2. An understanding of the necessity of turning one's life over to God, and thereby accepting Jesus Christ as Lord and Savior.

These, it seems to me, are the two foundation stones upon which everything else is built.

The Importance of the Group

Before we leave the subject of the Twelve Steps, I want to add that working through the steps in the context of a group can be immensely beneficial. Group therapy can serve the compulsive man in many ways. One of the most important of these ways is that it lets him know that he is not alone in his behavior. If you are in a group, you are going to see men who have come further along on the journey to wholeness than you have. That will encourage you to know that "if they can make it, so can I."

You will also probably have men in the group who have not made the sort of progress you have made. That, too, is encouraging, as their struggles will remind you of how far you *have* come.

Another reason why group therapy is so important is that it gives the typical "non-relational" male an opportunity to share his struggles in a supportive atmosphere. Men need to connect with other men who are becoming healthy. They need to retake their place among their brothers.

As John Bradshaw says: "To heal our toxic shame we must come out of hiding." We do this, he says, "by social contact, which means honestly sharing our feelings with significant others," and by "seeing ourselves mirrored and echoed in the eyes of at least one non-shaming person . . . Reestablishing an 'interpersonal bridge.' "[5]

Before we leave the Twelve Steps, I want to remind you to be thorough in your completion of each, and be patient, especially with yourself. As Patrick Carnes says, "There are no magic solutions—only time and constant use of [Twelve-Step] program principles."[6]

With time and patience, the miracle of new strength will certainly come.

11
GROWING IN SPIRITUAL HEALTH

Michael virtually glared at me when I asked him about his relationship with Christ.

"Don't tell me that I need to receive Christ," he said. "I did that years ago. I know all about being born again!"

"Oh," I said. "I apologize if I've offended you. I didn't realize that you were a Christian."

"Yes, sir," he said, still a bit angry. "I accepted Christ at youth camp when I must have been . . . oh . . . nine years old."

I nodded and smiled as I wondered how to suggest that it was time for Michael to "receive Christ" again. His Christianity was related to something that had happened nearly thirty years ago. As far as I could see, it had no bearing on the life he was living today. He spoke of his relationship with Jesus as if it were a nostalgic memory—and not a living reality of his day-to-day existence.

And I knew that, more than anything else, what Michael really needed was the reality of the Lord's presence in his life.

I am afraid that far too many people, even those who think they are Christians, have done with Christ exactly what Michael did with Him. They have left Him behind, like some relic of childhood. If you ask them if they know Jesus, the answer is immediate: "Oh yes, of course." But the reality is that He is someone they *used* to know. If they are honest with themselves, most men, and especially those who struggle with compulsive behavior, would have to admit that they have a decided poverty of spirit and a meager inner life.

It is time to receive Jesus again.

It is time to invite Him into every area of our lives, to allow His love and grace to permeate everything we do and everything we are.

It is time to return to the childlike faith of the little boy who accepted Christ in camp all those years ago—or who went down to the altar that Sunday morning so long ago, determined that he would always live for His Lord—or who was so thrilled by the Bible stories his mother read him at bedtime that he thought seriously about becoming a missionary when he grew up. Do you see yourself in any of those little boys? If so, it's time to go back to that simpler time, when you knew that Jesus cared, and that He was ready and anxious to love away any hurt that came into your life.

If you never knew Jesus in that way when you were a child, it is still not too late for you to know him that way now!

Please don't be offended, as Michael was, when I suggest that it is time for you to receive Christ again. Perhaps you have always lived close to Christ, and feel that you couldn't possibly be any closer to Him than you are right now. If that's the way it is with you, that is terrific! But that's not at all the way it is for most of us.

You see, most of us have come to think of giving our lives to Christ as a once-and-for-all thing. You do it once, and then you never have to worry about it again—and there is a sense in which that is true. Once you have accepted Christ as Lord and Savior, you have received salvation, and you will never have to receive salvation again.

But there is also a sense in which Christ must be accepted again and again and again, and that is what I am talking about right now. Actually, it involves a process of learning how to be yielded to Christ on a daily basis and the practice of living in His grace.

Receiving Christ means to live in His love—to understand that we are beings created in the image of God, and that God thinks so much of us that He sent Christ to die for us. When Christ truly lives within, we can stop hating ourselves (as many compulsive men do), and understand that it's perfectly all right to be a human being.

I like this quote from Leanne Payne: "We do not climb a ladder of knowledge, goodness, or good works to get to God. Any such mode bypasses the Incarnation and the Cross. Rather, Christ descends to us and into us. He incarnates us. We are indwelt, ingodded."[1]

The compulsive male needs to understand that his identity is rooted in Christ. In Christ, he is whole and complete, lacking nothing. Outside of Christ, he can do nothing at all.

"To speak of the true self, of personality at all—that is, of man as fully human—is to speak of man's fellowship with God and with others."[2]

Receiving Jesus Into Your Shame

If you want to be completely whole, then you must invite Jesus into the areas of your life that cause you grief or pain, directly into your shame.

The prime way to bring Jesus into your shame is to acknowledge that you are a human being. You are not subhuman, nor are you superhuman. You are, simply, a man. And the incarnation of Christ proved God's love for us, because through the birth of Christ, He became human, too.

Instead of rejecting our humanity, we can rejoice in the knowledge that, as Christ ascended into heaven, He took a little bit of humanity with Him. Since we are made in the Father's image and recreated by faith in Christ's image, we can actually feel very good about being simply human. We are, after all, just "a little bit lower than the angels."[3]

Allowing Jesus into your shame is an act of faith, which recognizes that the time for self-hatred and self-rejection is over, that it is time to leave the guilt and shame *of* the past *in* the past, and move on into the future.

Whatever has happened in your past may be unbelievably horrible. You may have gone through the sort of tragedy that would cause the strongest man to cry and an ordinary man to give up on life. You may have caused some terrible tragedy to occur—or you may *believe* you caused some tragedy to occur, whether you were responsible or not.

Whatever happened back there that has caused you so much shame, Jesus can deal with it so that you never have to look at it again. You never have to think about it again. You can leave it completely alone. You just have to let it be and know that the grace of Christ is sufficient to cover it.

TED

Whenever I think of Jesus entering into someone's shame, I remember a man named Ted.

Ted was a big man, who weighed well over two hundred pounds. He regularly drank a case or two of beer over the weekend. He'd start drinking as soon as he got home from work on Friday, and keep on drinking until bedtime Sunday night.

One Friday night, Ted was sitting in front of the television set, watching the movie *Aliens* with his two boys, Jimmy and Barry, who were six and nine. He had already consumed a case of beer, and was absent-mindedly cleaning his .45 automatic pistol.

As the horror movie continued, the two boys starting scaring each other by yelling "Boo!" during the most tense moments of the movie. Ted joined in the fun, aiming his gun at the TV and pretending to shoot at the aliens whenever one of the monsters came on screen.

Everyone was having a good time, especially Jimmy, who giggled and laughed at the way his daddy was being so funny.

Then, during a lull in the action, the little boy suddenly jumped out in front of Ted and screamed, "Boo, Daddy!" and giggled uproariously.

In response, Ted aimed his gun at Jimmy's head and pulled the trigger.

Instead of the click he expected to hear, Ted's ears were

filled with the sound of gunfire.

Jimmy was thrown all the way across the room by the force of the impact. Shot in the head from such close range by such a large caliber bullet, there was no hope for Jimmy. By the time Ted was able to jump up and rush across the room, the little boy was dead.

As you can imagine, Ted was overwhelmed by grief and remorse over what he had done. Over and over and over, he kept replaying the moment in his mind, wishing to God he had *never* had all that beer, that he had never aimed that gun at his son, that he had never even *heard* of the movie *Aliens*. He could not get the image out of his mind—his little boy's eyes wide open in shock, his mouth suddenly gone from giggle to horror as the bullet took his life. But no matter how much he went over the incident in his mind, there was no way at all for Ted to go back into the past and undo the terrible tragedy that he had caused to happen.

I came to know Ted when I was working in a secular drug-and-alcohol rehabilitation center, where I was not supposed to "proselytize" recovering addicts or try to talk to them about Christ.

But when I saw what terrible anguish he was in, I immediately knew that there was only one way for him to be set free, and that was through the healing love of Christ. So in one of our sessions I asked him if he believed in God. He replied that he had been raised in a church-going home, but that he hadn't attended church in years. Church was one of those things he had left behind as he grew into adulthood—and God right along with it.

I knew that no secular technique or self-help system could alleviate this man's profound guilt. No recovery "system" could touch a wound of this nature. It was absolutely essential that Ted should come to know Christ, because only the Prince of Peace could bring peace to Ted's troubled and tormented soul.

I knew that I would have to represent the heart of God to this tormented person. It didn't matter whether I was "supposed" to share my faith. Christ's love was the only answer to Ted's shame and guilt. When the right moment arrived, I whispered a silent prayer that God would help me find the right words that would help Ted open his heart to Christ.

But Ted had a problem accepting Christ's love, because he felt so ashamed of himself. "I know He'll never forgive what I did to my son," he said. Then he began to cry.

"Well, what would you say to Jesus if He were right here in the room with us?" I asked. "If you could just sit down and talk to Him . . . face-to-face?"

"I'm so sorry . . . I'm so sorry . . . please help me, Lord!" He began to weep, quietly at first, and then in great, heaving sobs.

"Ted," I said quietly. "You know that Jesus loves you . . . don't you?"

He nodded in response.

"If you could hear His voice, I know He would tell you that He suffered on the cross for you. He would say something like, 'I am taking your sins upon myself. I am being made a sacrifice for sin to my heavenly Father. I am paying the price for all your sins. I love you and I forgive you. Give your heart to me, follow me, and I will heal you. I love you.' That's what He would say to you."

I knew that the things I said were the sort of words that would come directly from the heart of Jesus to bring peace and healing to this broken, desperate man.

Ted began to wail, he was so overcome with grief. He cried from the core of his being, with tears streaming down his contorted and repentant face. His shoulders shook and heaved. There was something deeply healing about the way he was crying. I had seen him cry before, but it was always because of the pain of remembering what he had done—how he had pulled the trigger that ended the life of his little boy.

This time he was crying because he was receiving forgiveness.

When his tears slowed down a bit, I asked him if he wanted to accept Jesus into his life and become a Christian. He nodded and said that yes, he did. I asked him to repeat this prayer aloud if he believed the words I was saying. I then led him through a "sinner's prayer."

"Dear Jesus, I know I am a sinner. I believe that you are the only Son of God and that you died for my sins. Please forgive me and make me your child. I give my life to you, help me follow your will. Amen."

He choked out the words through his tears.

He had received Christ into his shame and he had been healed.

Ted did receive healing on that day. It didn't erase what had happened to Jimmy, but it did make the pain bearable. And Ted also found that there is Love at work in the universe that is able to work things out for those who are willing to surrender to Him. What happened can't be changed, but one day, as God's perfect plan for the universe unfolds, even the worst things that have happened to us will be made all right.

As the Bible says: "God himself will be with them and be their God. He will wipe every tear from their eyes. There will be no more death or mourning or crying or pain, for the old order of things has passed away."[4]

One day, God will wipe away the tears from the eyes of *all* of His people. He can wipe away *your* tears today . . . if only you'll let him. Will Jesus come into your shame? Of course He will. All you have to do is issue the invitation:

"Dear Lord. I have done so many things in my life that I'm ashamed of. Sometimes it's hard for me to deal with my sense of guilt and shame. Jesus, I know that your death on the cross took away all my sins. Please help me to let you take away the guilt and shame I feel over those sins. Help me to live in freedom. I want to always remember, Jesus, that my guilt and shame have been washed away by your overwhelming love. Amen."

Jesus is always ready to listen to you, and your prayers can be much more specific than the one above. Whatever causes you shame, take it to Christ, talk to Him about it, and let Him deal with it. Like all the prayers in this book, the one I have written here is given merely as an example that can be modified in any way that you see necessary.

Receiving Jesus Into Your Anger

Most men are much angrier than they think they are. Yet, if you ask someone why he looks so mad, he'll probably respond by yelling at you, "I'm not mad! What are you talking about!"

He may even punch you in the nose just to make you understand that he's *not* angry!

But before a man can receive Jesus into his anger, he has to admit that he's angry—just as a man cannot receive forgiveness for his sins if he refuses to admit that he's a sinner.

Years of living with the frustrations of life can take their toll. The hurt you have experienced can cause anger to freeze somewhere inside of you.

Some men spend most of their time trying to suppress their anger because they are afraid of what the consequences will be if they give in to it.

I've mentioned it before, but it's worth repeating: There is nothing inherently wrong with anger. Jesus himself was enraged enough that He used a whip to drive the moneychangers out of the temple, and He often spoke angrily to those who were self-righteous and hypocritical.

Anger is an emotion—and like all emotions it can be used for good or bad. It can build. It can destroy. It can be a catalyst for changing unjust situations, and it can be a burning fire that destroys everything in its path. And I guarantee you, if you try to stuff your anger deep down inside of you and keep a lid on it, but never really deal with it . . . it will destroy *you.*

If you have a particular problem with anger, you must invite Jesus into the center of it so that He can bring you serenity and forgiveness.

You can do that by earnestly praying a prayer like this one:

"Dear Jesus, I know you experienced anger on earth. Please help me to feel my anger, to express it constructively without hurting anyone, and to confess it to you. Help me to stop swallowing, eating, or 'compulsing' my behavior away. I ask you to heal my anger so that I don't need to medicate myself to soothe it. And Lord, please teach me how to be angry without sinning. Amen."

Receiving Jesus Into Your Grief

"Jesus wept."[5]

This verse—the Bible's shortest verse—from the Gospel of John, has a great deal to say. It tells us that "real men" can and do cry. That they do not have to stuff their sadness deep down inside of them so that no one else will ever see it.

Mike couldn't understand why he was so depressed. He had a good, secure job, a loving wife, and three well-behaved and intelligent children. He was thirty-five years old, so he should have been at the prime of his life.

But something was wrong, and other people noticed it. They sometimes commented on how sad he looked. All Mike knew was that he was less interested in others these days, felt discouraged about the future, and had trouble sleeping.

He didn't know why he felt that way, and, frankly, he was kind of scared. It seemed that this sadness was overpowering him. He would sometimes find himself on the verge of tears for no reason at all. And then, one night while watching the movie *Field of Dreams*, he broke down and began to sob uncontrollably. His crying lasted for over an hour.

Through counseling, Mike and I came to see that his grief had much to do with his relationship with his father. His dad had been very critical of him when he was growing up, and then had died while Mike was still in his teens. He didn't remember if he cried at his father's funeral or not. He just didn't feel much of anything when the man died.

Mike had repressed his sadness for more than twenty years when it finally reached out and grabbed hold of him, nearly choking the life out of him.

Once Mike came to realize what was going on in his life, he began to pray that God would help him handle his grief in the proper way. In essence, he "gave permission" to God to bring his grief to the surface of his life, and he told Jesus that he would not try to hold back his tears any longer. If God wanted him to cry, he would cry.

For three days, on and off, he wept silently and allowed himself to grieve. By giving himself permission to let the tears flow, and by receiving Jesus into his grief, Mike was able to receive the transforming power of God's grace. Instead of allowing the sadness to harden into depression, he received healing because he was willing to feel his own pain and to ask Jesus to come into it.

Perhaps you can't identify with someone like Mike, so full of grief over what should have been but never was. But then again, perhaps you understand *exactly* how he felt.

In any case, because we live on a fallen planet—a planet that, due to sin, is not the way God intended it to be—many things happen to all of us that make us sad. But sadness should be felt, dealt with, and surrendered to Christ's love. It should not be shoved down inside, where it will grow to unmanageable proportions and threaten to drown you.

If you can't seem to feel your sadness, but others are always asking you what's wrong, I suggest you pray a prayer like this one:

"Lord Jesus, please help me to feel the sadness that may be in me. And help me surrender that sadness to you, knowing that you are the Lord who washes away all tears from the eyes of His people. Touch me, and heal me, I pray, and help me to live every moment of my life close to you. Amen."

To be a real man does not mean to be totally free from emotions like shame, anger, or grief. To be a real man means to be honest about our emotions and to accept them as part of the fabric of life.

You see, it is the great irony of manhood—true manhood—that to become strong we must embrace our weakness. To become "poor in spirit." When we recognize our powerlessness, our emptiness without Christ—only then do we begin to live in true relationship with the one who completes us as men in the depths of our being.

He is the one who leads us to the place where, finally, we can retake our manhood.

12

RETAKING OUR MANHOOD

Spiritual growth is full of amazing and sometimes confusing paradoxes such as, "To gain your life you must lose it."

In the course of this book, we've uncovered a number of other paradoxes—basic truths that seem to go against the traditional wisdom of the world.

For example, from a worldly perspective, it would seem to make sense that you should stuff your anger down inside and keep a lid on it. That's just the civil thing to do. But the truth is that only by facing up to your anger and letting it out will you eventually come to peace and wholeness.

Another sensible thing to do, it seems, would be to try harder to overcome whatever compulsive behavior has you bound. Just grit your teeth and do it. Unfortunately "trying harder" only works for a season, and the compulsion almost always comes back stronger than ever. The truth is that it's only through surrender, through facing your own powerlessness over whatever compulsion has you bound, that you can finally be set free.

Another paradox: The world says, "What you don't know can't hurt you," but we have discovered that the opposite is true. What you don't know *can* hurt you. Not only hurt you, but destroy you. All those things that you've hidden from yourself have to be faced up to for you to become the man you'd really like to be, the man God intends for you to be. If you honestly don't know why you do what you do—then you're probably going to keep right on doing it. But once you understand that your compulsive behavior is only covering up some long-hidden pain, you can deal with the pain itself, and you'll no longer have need of the compulsive behavior.

It is important that you come to know the reason for your anger, your shame, your grief—that you face it head on and deal with it. Once you've done that, and once you've invited Jesus into every area of your life, you will be able to stop "medicating" your pain through excessive doses of alcohol, drugs, sex, work, or any other compulsion.

It's not easy to face up to inner pain, I realize that. But the person who is numb to his pain is almost always numb to every other area of life as well. He cannot truly feel pleasure, exhilaration, joy, or love. He is truly passionless. He is emotionally dead. And that is a terrible, terrible price to pay to escape from emotional pain—no matter how intense that pain might be.

But through the healing love of Christ, the one who is emotionally dead can come to experience spiritual resurrection—an awakening to full manhood.

Jesus and Resurrected Manhood

I am often asked, "Don't you think that Jesus alone is sufficient?"

Certainly I do.

"Then why do we need to understand all these psychological principles?"

This question shows a lack of understanding about what psychology is and does.

You may remember what happened in California a few years ago when the parents of a diabetic son decided that God alone could heal their boy. They threw his insulin away and refused to go back to it even after they saw that he was becoming weaker and sicker with every passing hour. They believed that Jesus was all their son needed, and that using medicine was simply a sign of a lack of faith.

Unfortunately, their son died—and his parents wound up in court, facing charges of child abuse. How sad that this little boy had to pay the ultimate price for his parents' lack of understanding.

In fact, those people were being presumptuous. Yes, Jesus Christ created the human body, and yes He is capable of healing with a word or a touch. But He is also the One who gave us medicines and doctors. Very few among us would refuse to go to the doctor if we were really sick.

Just as Jesus created the human body, He also created the human spirit. Nobody understands the way our spirits work better than Jesus does. As you read through the New Testament, you'll see that Christ actually practiced quite a bit of psychology during His earthly ministry.

Jesus often spoke of the human spirit, or *psyche,* when He talked about the prime importance of heart-motive in all that we do. Again and again, He insisted that what goes on deep down inside of a man is what's most important to God.

Just as God gave us doctors and medicines to use when the body is sick, I believe He also gave us the insights into the human spirit—including our mind and emotions—that are being used so effectively by many psychologists today.

True, there are some types of psychology that are nothing more than philosophy in disguise, and as such they may be in conflict with evangelical theology. But there are other aspects of psychology—childhood development, for instance—that have been examined, tested, and tried as thoroughly as any other science, and have proved to be true and accurate beyond any doubt.

Here is my point in revisiting this discussion about psychology at the close of this book: Even men who truly want to be released from sins and compulsions can have a negative reaction when they feel that someone is "prying" inside them. Many of us put up incredible resistance, and all manner of barriers—anything to keep another person from knowing what is happening in the depths of our soul.

Let me ask: Are you also resisting the Holy Spirit when He wants to speak to you about the brokenness of your inner man—the real you who exists behind the casual facade? Have you been thinking that you should "clean up your act" *before* you come to God and ask Him to help you? If so, then you may be falling into the old trap of the self-righteous, trying to make yourself presentable to the loving Father who has said to us through Jesus, "Come to me all you who are weary and burdened . . . and you will find rest for your souls" (Matthew 11:28, 29).

It is ironic to me that so many men insist they are Christians—who believe the Bible "cover to cover"—and yet they have not discovered the green pastures and still waters that the Shepherd of our souls wants to lead us to. Instead, they continue to live entombed in their own fallen pride and opinion and self-sufficiency.

As a brother in Christ, and as one who must continually depend on the Holy Spirit to help me live free of compulsions that would bind me, I want to ask you: Have you made Jesus Lord of your life—that is, of your outward affairs—but not allowed Him full access to your spirit?

In fact, many of the people who have come to me for help were unable to receive Christ's grace due to their past experiences or behavioral problems, until, through counseling, we brought down all the barriers. To my delight, I have found that many psychological principles can help a man open the doors of his heart so that he can accept Christ and all that He has to offer.

I would never attempt to use psychology without Christ—but I also know that combined with prayer, psychological counseling can bring about wonderful new growth in a man's life.

No More Pretending

In his book *Inside Out,* Larry Crabb writes, "Most of us cope with life by pretending. We pretend that what we have satisfies more than it does. And we pretend that we haven't been hurt as badly as we have. . . . Many people have been trained in conservative churches and Christian families to deny that they hurt . . . to deal with what's really going on inside is disturbing, too uncomfortable; so we hide the inside truth from others—and from ourself."[1]

And yet, unless we allow ourselves to feel our own pain, we will not be able to move into the wholeness that God has planned for us.

Bringing Jesus into the very core of your shamed self is to allow His life-giving Spirit to transform your pain into a fount of character-building water.

The only way you can retake your manhood is to reject the momentary salves that may alleviate your existential pain temporarily, but which will ultimately leave you feeling thirstier than ever. You can only regain mastery over the inner man by coming to re-identify with the God-Man, Jesus Christ. And if you are a Christian, He is alive inside of you through His Holy and Life-Giving Spirit.

It is time for us, as men, to take the initiative to retake our intimate relationships with our wives, our children, and our friends. The simple first step for retaking these relationships is to stop pretending that it doesn't hurt when it does, to begin to identify your feelings and to talk about them to someone you can trust.

As we begin to realize the ways in which we have been estranged emotionally from ourselves, our wives, and our children, we will see that we have also been estranged from other men. Retaking our place among our brothers will be a high priority.

Men who have had insufficient male role models in their formative years tend to become especially distrustful, competitive, and distant from other men. But what a poverty of soul to have no close male confidants.

Men need to build bridges toward other men because there are things that only a man can give to another man. Retaking our manhood means reconnecting with other men who are also fellow sojourners. Instead of shaming other men or competing with them, or even ignoring them, we are called to embrace them.

Just as a healthy man will make a better husband, or a better friend, he will also make a more effective parent. Unless a man begins to realize that he is just as dysfunctional as his father before him was, he is likely going to pass along a negative and hurtful heritage to his own sons and daughters. A healthy, growing male will rethink his approach to parenting and evaluate how he interacts with his children. He will learn to talk to his children and share with them—not scream at them, criticize them, or ignore them.

Retaking your manhood means to become proactive. Instead of reacting to life, instead of doing nothing and watching things go from bad to worse, you must take action to regain your wounded masculinity.

To retake your manhood, you can:

1. Stop denying your pain.
2. Recognize that to be human means to have sadness and anger.
3. Learn to identify your feelings.
4. Experience relationship by sharing verbally your pain with others.
5. Stop "medicating your pain" with destructive compulsions.
6. Develop an inner life and a Christian spirituality founded on God's grace in Christ and self-acceptance.
7. Stop shaming yourself and others for being human. Stop blaming others for your problems.
8. Accept the fact that the greatest problem in your life is yourself and your own refusal to accept life on life's terms.
9. Become accountable to other men and stop isolating yourself from close relationships with them.
10. In prayer, allow God daily—and moment by moment—to walk with you through the pain—until you are living at rest in Him (Hebrews 4:1, 2).

The old thinking about what it means to be a man must be left behind. It is time for all of us men to look within ourselves and face the pain that we encounter there.

Although this may be difficult to do, in time, with His grace, our unfinished manhood can be transformed into something that will truly bless our friends, our families—and our Creator.

ACKNOWLEDGMENTS

I would like to acknowledge the following people for the teaching, knowledge, support, and love that I have received from them.

First, I'd like to acknowledge the following ministers: The Rev. Larry Reinertson and all the members of Narberth Presbyterian Church, who worshiped together from 1978 through 1984; The Rev. Len Pure and all the Members of Full Gospel Word Fellowship who worshiped together from 1984 through 1986, and the clergy and people of The Church of The Good Samaritan. Thank you all for your love and witness.

Special thanks to the Rev. Ian Scott, chaplain of Eastern College, for his encouraging support in my early student ministry. To all the scattered supporters of the Full Gospel Fellowship from Eastern College—thank you, wherever you may be!

Of the many fine psychiatrists, psychologists, and psychotherapists who have trained and supervised me, I would especially like to thank Dr. Richard P. Fitzgibbons, M.D.

Also, Dr. Jim Collins, Ed.D. and the Rev. Frank Kaemingk of Christian Counseling and Guidance Services in Denver. Of my Denver Seminary professors, a special thanks to Dr. Charles Raup and Dr. Jim Beck along with Dr. Craig Blomberg.

Special acknowledgment to Ms. Carmen Hartman, C.A.C. for teaching me about addictions.

I would also like to thank Bethany House Publishers, especially David Hazard and Mrs. Carol Johnson.

154 / Three Compulsions That Defeat Most Men

Special thanks to Dr. Thomas Whiteman, Ph.D. and all the staff at Life Counseling Services.

A special thanks to Glen Covert. "There is a friend who sticks closer than a brother."

Thank you to my family for their support.

NOTES

CHAPTER TWO

1. Reuben Fine, *Troubled Men* (San Francisco: Josey-Bass, Inc., 1988), p. 305.

2. John Bradshaw, *Healing the Shame That Binds You* (Deerfield Beach, Fla.: Health Communications Inc., 1988), p. 69.

CHAPTER THREE

1. James 5:16.

2. Galatians 5:19–21.

3. M. Scott Peck, *The Road Less Traveled* (New York: Simon and Schuster, 1978), p. 16.

4. Bradshaw, *Healing the Shame That Binds You,* p. 15.

CHAPTER FIVE

1. Dr. Patrick Carnes, *Don't Call It Love* (New York: Bantam Books, 1991), p. 104.

2. Carnes, *Don't Call It Love,* p. 15.

3. Carnes, pp. 67, 68.

4. Peter Trachtenberg, *The Casanova Complex* (New York: Poseidon Press, 1988), p. 19.

5. Trachtenberg, *The Casanova Complex,* p. 74.

6. Romans 12:1.

7. From Sexaholics Anonymous literature.

CHAPTER SIX

1. Michael Elkin, *Families Under the Influence* (New York: W. W. Norton and Company, 1984), p. 42.

2. For an in-depth discussion of physical problems associated with the consumption of alcohol, see Allen Luks and Joseph Barbato, *You Are What You Drink* (New York: Stonesong Press, 1989)

3. 1 Corinthians 10:12.

4. Elkin, *Families Under the Influence*, p. 58.

5. Elkin, p. 57.

6. Drs. Robert Hemfelt, Frank Minirth, and Paul Meier, *Love Is a Choice* (Nashville: Thomas Nelson Publishers, 1989), pp. 72, 73.

7. Ephesians 5:18.

CHAPTER SEVEN

1. Jane Middleton-Moz, *Shame and Guilt: Masters of Disguise* (Deerfield Beach, Fla.: Health Communications, Inc., 1990), p. 14.

2. 1 Corinthians 7:10.

3. Middleton-Moz, *Shame and Guilt: Masters of Disguise*, p. 62.

4. Middleton-Moz, p. 46.

5. Middleton-Moz, pp. xii, xiii.

6. Hemfelt, *et. al.*, *Love Is a Choice*, p. 172.

7. Hemfelt, p. 105.

8. From Co-Dependency Worksheet, author unknown.

9. Hemfelt, p. 11.

10. Hemfelt, pp. 11, 12.

11. Middleton-Moz, p. 78.

12. Philippians 4:7.

13. Hemfelt, p. 173.

CHAPTER EIGHT

1. James 4:6.

2. Trachtenberg, *The Casanova Complex*, p. 29.

3. Matthew 11:28–30

4. Hemfelt, *Love Is a Choice*, p. 139.

CHAPTER TEN

1. Ephesians 4:27.

2. Bernard Green, *Getting Over Getting High* (New York: William Morrow and Company, 1985), p. 204.

3. Hebrews 4:15.

4. Carnes, *Don't Call It Love,* pp. 322, 323.

5. Bradshaw, *Healing the Shame That Binds You,* p. 115.

8. Carnes, p. 217.

CHAPTER ELEVEN

1. Leanne Payne, *The Healing Presence* (Wheaton, Ill.: Crossway Books, 1989), p. 79.

2. Payne, p. 51.

3. Psalm 8:5.

4. Revelation 21:3, 4.

5. John 11:35.

CHAPTER TWELVE

1. Larry Crabb, *Inside Out* (Colorado Springs: Navpress, 1988), p. 89.